West Norfolk and King's Lynn

High School for Girls

1886 to 1979

Michael Walker

King's Lynn

First published in Great Britain in 2012 by
K.E.S. Publications
King Edward VII School
Gaywood Road
King's Lynn
PE30 4ER

Typeset in Times New Roman and printed by
DSD Colour Printers, King's Lynn.

A catalogue record for this book is available from the British Library.

ISBN 978-0-9565697-1-4

Contents

Introduction

Having written two books about the history of King Edward VII School, I decided that the girls had been sadly neglected and that I should attempt to redress the balance. There have been brief accounts of the school's history published in the past, for example in the 1937 edition of the School Magazine and in a special edition published to mark the 75th anniversary, *The King's Lynn High School, 1886 – 1962*. In addition, when the King Street building was finally closed in 1985, a grand re-union was held and a booklet was produced entitled, *The West Norfolk and King's Lynn High School for Girls, 1887 – 1979*. Unfortunately the latter has no indication of authorship. All three of these contain reminiscences by former pupils and staff. Margaret Lewis who edited the 1962 booklet acknowledged the work done by Miss Dore and Miss Passmore in collecting the contributions, some of which were from alumnae who had been at the school as early as the 1900s. I have drawn on those reminiscences as well as on others especially collected for this book. In addition I have used posts on the High School pages on the *West Norfolk Forum* and on *Facebook* and quoted from them to illustrate different recollections and viewpoints.

One over-riding impression I have gained from reading the various reminiscences is that the girls, for the most part, enjoyed their time at the High School. To quote just one correspondent, Mrs Shirley Bowler (Dexter) at the school from 1960 to 1965, 'They say school days are the happiest days of your life and I can certainly say that I enjoyed every moment there. All the teachers were so helpful and approachable.' Of course not everyone would agree with that sentiment and contrary views are expressed in the book.

Among the other main resources used have been four scrapbooks which were kept for the whole of the period from 1886 to 1979. They include photographs, newspaper cuttings, copies of letters and various documents, prize-giving programmes and prospectuses. Perhaps the most important of the four was compiled by Mr G H Anderson who was Clerk to the Governors for over fifty years. In addition I have also had access to Governors' minutes, an almost complete set of School Magazines, HMI Reports, Examination Results and a range of other documents.

As well as describing the history of the school in terms of numbers on roll, the development of the buildings, organisation and curriculum, examination results, extra-curricular activities and the influence of the Head Mistresses and staff, I have tried to identify students who were successful in a wide range of fields – academically, in sport, in drama, in music and in various competitions. Unfortunately it is impossible to mention every former student or teacher and inevitably many who deserve a mention may have been omitted. For that I apologise.

I very much hope that readers will find the story as interesting as I have. Hopefully the text and the photographs will evoke many happy memories.

Michael Walker

February 2012

Acknowledgements

I am particularly grateful to the staff at Springwood High School, especially to Andy Johnson, the Head Teacher, for access to the High School documents which have been preserved at the school since 1979. My sincere thanks go to all the many former students who have loaned me photographs and/or have written accounts of their time at the school. Hopefully these reminiscences, together with those gleaned from earlier publications, will bring the book alive for its readers. I am also grateful to the Norfolk Record Office for permission to reproduce extracts from relevant documents, specifically the Governors' Minutes and the private papers of Audrey Stratford and Grace Leeder.

It has not been possible to trace the sources of all the photographs. Where known they are acknowledged. In some cases the companies, such as Panora, Jewsons and Goodchild, are no longer in business but many of the photographs of groups were taken by them. I am very grateful to the *Lynn News* and the *EDP* for permission to reproduce photographs which originally appeared in the press, to Brenda Lance (Roy) for her skill in improving the quality of many of the older photographs, to Robert Fuller for his help with photographs and to Tim Steer and my wife Elizabeth who have read the script and made helpful suggestions. Finally my thanks go to Jane Whiskens at DSD Colour Printers for her skill in setting the text and the photographs.

The Author

Michael Walker began his teaching career in the West Riding of Yorkshire. Following that, for eight years, he was the Geography Tutor in the University of Oxford Department of Educational Studies, during which time he wrote a number of successful Geography textbooks and taught part-time in two local schools. After six years as a Deputy Head in an Oxfordshire comprehensive school he was a Head for twenty years, firstly at Buxton College in Derbyshire and then, from 1990, at King Edward VII School in King's Lynn. Following his retirement from the headship in 2002 he worked on a number of school leadership programmes as a National College Consultant. In recent years he has published two books on the history of King Edward VII School:

King Edward VII School, A Centenary Celebration, Book Guild Publishing, 2005.

Diary of a Grammar School, King's Lynn, K.E.S. Publications, 2010.

1. 1886-89. A faltering beginning.

Although in some documents the school is said to date from 1887 it actually began in 1886 as the Eastern Centre of a group of schools run by the Graduated County Schools' Association (GCSA). This had been formed as a limited company in 1884 to 'to establish and conduct Boarding and Day Schools or Colleges for the general (including technical and religious) education and training of boys and girls.' The Chairman of the company was the Reverend J L Brereton, a Prebendary of Exeter Cathedral and the Rector of Little Massingham, who was well known for his work in education. One of the school Houses was later named after him.

In January 1886 the Reverend Brereton acquired a private school previously run by the late Madame Goebbels in St Margaret's House:

Lynn

January 6th 1886

Dear Sir

I am glad to accept the terms on which you propose to transfer to me the Ladies' School at St Margaret's Place.

May I ask you to convey to the parents who have girls at the school my assurance that I will do my best to provide all that they may wish for the care and teaching of their children during the next term which is to commence on the 26th instant.

The process of turning a private school into a public school requires much careful consideration and the cordial co-operation of others. I trust that before Easter much will have been done to ensure the permanent confidence of the inhabitants of Lynn and the neighbourhood in what will now become the first 'County School for Girls' established in the East of England.

I am,

Yours faithfully

J L Brereton

Monsieur Goebbels

At a public meeting held on 8 January at the Town Hall and chaired by the Mayor, Mr J D Thew, the proposal to establish in King's Lynn a school for girls received a good level of support. Shortly after the meeting a prospectus was issued indicating that the new school would open on 26 January 1886, a date which from the 1950s was commemorated as Founder's Day. The school was initially based in St Margaret's House but by the middle of 1886 it had moved to the large house at 11 King Street known as the Trenowath Rooms and this was to be its base until January 1903.

A prospectus issued for the new term in September 1886 lists Miss Bannister as the Head Mistress and Miss Thompson as Second Mistress. The fees were £14 per term for boarders and three guineas for day pupils. Termly charges for advanced classes were five guineas and for the preparatory school (for boys and girls aged 4 to 8 years,) two guineas. If the little boys were

The Trenowath Building at 11 King Street

taught Latin there was an additional charge of one guinea per term. At this stage the fees were not all inclusive. Books could be bought from the school and for stationery there was an additional charge of 5s per term.

On 14 September 1886 an examination was held at the GCSA's four centres. At each of the schools there were two scholarships worth £20, which were only open to boarders, four of £10 and four of £5, the latter available only to day girls. By May 1887 the GCSA had opened ten schools in different parts of the country but it obviously overreached itself and it went into liquidation on 28 June 1887.

There was much concern in the town about the future of the Girls' School and following meetings held in King's Lynn in July it was decided that a new company, the Girls' County School Association Ltd, would be formed to ensure that it would not close. New share capital was raised which allowed the continuance of the school in the Trenowath Building. The first Prospectus lists the Reverend Henry Smith, HM Inspector of Schools, as Chairman of the Board of Directors, Mr C B Plowright as Vice Chairman and Mr G H Anderson as Clerk. The latter was to continue in a similar capacity until January 1940. Other Directors included such well known local people as Mrs Eva Cresswell, Mrs Plowright, Mr E M Beloe, Mr A Jermyn and Mr W Hitchcock. Miss Bannister remained as Head Mistress under the new arrangement and was assisted by three other resident staff, Miss Leahy (who had studied Mathematics at Girton College), Miss Mead (English, History and Modern Languages) and Miss Bold (Art and Music). Like Miss Bannister, Miss Bold had taught at Worcester Park in London, one of the original GCSA schools. She was to teach at the school until 1919.

At the First Annual General Meeting of the new company in February 1888 Mr Plowright, who was in the Chair, said 'The Directors are glad to report that the efforts to keep open the County School for Girls in Lynn have been fully justified by the results of the first term….The fact that during the term there were 49 pupils clearly shows that such a school was required, and the accounts presented herewith prove that it can be carried on with financial success.' The profit for the term was £19.11s.1d. At the same meeting it was decided to change the name from *The County School for Girls* to *The High School for Girls*.

In July of 1888 the school held its first Prize Giving in the Assembly Rooms at the Town Hall and, according to the *Lynn News*, it was attended by 'a numerous company of ladies and gentlemen'. Perhaps the most important announcement was that the Princess of Wales had agreed to give a Prize for Good Conduct. The Prince of Wales had, since 1864, presented a Gold Medal each year to the most academically successful student at the Lynn Grammar School and one can assume that the Princess was persuaded that a parallel prize at the High School for Girls was appropriate. After Edward VII came to the throne in 1901 it became known as the Queen's Prize and has been awarded in turn by Queen Alexandra, Queen Mary and the two Queen Elizabeths.

To return to 1888, other ladies had followed the example set by the Princess of Wales and donated the remainder of the prizes. The first recipient of the Good Conduct Prize was Gertrude Swann. The practice of asking ladies to donate prizes continued until 1892 when it was announced that the school was in such a flourishing condition that the Directors no longer needed to ask for this help. It was stressed that this did not apply to the prize donated by the Princess of Wales which was clearly seen in a different light from the others.

Prize Giving or Speech Days, as they were to be known in later years, were to become an important feature of the High School's year and were held annually except during the two World Wars. In 1888 Miss Bannister reported that the conduct of the girls was on the whole excellent. However she went on to make an extraordinary statement about their attitude to work:

'The pupils in the school think that they work very hard. Whether this is the case or not, they do not suffer from overwork, nor are they likely to do so as long as they are as ready as they are at present to ask for redress of grievances when pressure of work is making itself felt.'

This was a rather sour remark to make so publicly. However she did realise the importance of relaxation and identified a major problem which would not get addressed for some years, the lack of space for recreation:

'It is a matter for great regret that our scope for playing well is so restricted by lack of space....one of the things earnestly to be desired for the future is a good playground or garden, where relaxation from work will be possible for mistresses and pupils.'

At the second such occasion, held in August 1889, again in the Town Hall Assembly Rooms, the Chairman, the Reverend Henry Smith, praised the work of Miss Bannister who had left at the end of the summer term. He said that they were losing an excellent Head Mistress and that the school would never have reached its present position had it not been for her untiring efforts. Numbers were steadily increasing, up from 49 the previous year to 57 and it was expected that there would be even more on roll in the coming term. The number of successful examination candidates was also up from six (out of seven entries) in 1888 to 27 out of 31 in 1889. At this early stage in the school's history the girls were entered for a variety of examinations, including those of the Cambridge Locals Board, the College of Preceptors, Trinity College of Music and the South Kensington College of Art.

In a rather telling remark the Chairman said that the school 'as was said the previous day of the Grammar School....was on an upward plane. Like that school they had had many difficulties to contend with; they inherited a bad name, but they intend to earn a good one.' The comment about the school's bad name presumably refers to the fact that the original company had gone into liquidation. His reference to the Lynn Grammar School does however need some explanation. In 1887 the Head Master, the Reverend J B Slight, had been declared bankrupt and this had greatly disrupted the work of the school. One consequence was that the Prince of Wales Gold Medal was not awarded in 1887 and 1888. Fortunately both schools from this point would develop and become very successful.

Miss Ethel Waldegrave who was a pupil at the school when it started its life in the Trenowath Rooms, and later a junior-form teacher for 37 years from 1898 to the end of 1935, remembered Miss Bannister 'as a very dignified little lady, dressed in black silk and a lace cap'. Like many school pupils she thought the Head Mistress was much older than she was: 'I believe she was about thirty years old, but she seemed to us at least sixty.' She remembered the atmosphere in the school as being very subdued. There was no playtime, only a short break for lunch. 'Talking was strictly forbidden on the landings and in the entrance hall and in fact nearly everywhere.' The penalty for talking was the loss of order marks which had to be owned up to in each morning after prayers and roll call.

An even more graphic account of the school in those early days was provided by Mrs Charles Webb, (Mabel Howell), the Queens' Prize winner in 1892, in an article in the School Magazine in 1930, extracts from which are reproduced below:

'The prevailing atmosphere was of 'strict obedience and even repression….the things that one might not do were very clearly defined. There was an elaborate system of 'order marks' and a very rigid rule of silence which had to be maintained from the time of entering the long stone-flagged hall, where we changed our walking shoes, until we reached our own school room. The fine for disobedience was order marks, varying in number with the place in which this rule of silence had been broken. At the end of term these seemed to make an enormous total….

Miss Bannister was 'very frail looking and dressed always in black. She was very dignified and severe (or at least she seemed so to me)….

For Roll Call in the morning we all had to learn a verse from a chapter of the New Testament, and we were supposed to remember all of the chapter which had gone before. Anyone might be chosen to say the verse for the day and the penalty for failure to do so was, of course, an order mark.'

Things were very different when Miss Bannister left to get married and was replaced by Miss Harrison.

A copy of the Revd. Brereton's letter to M. Goebbels

2. 1889-1919. An enthusiast in education.

It seems that it was not possible to find a university graduate who was a suitable candidate as Head Mistress and so Miss Edith M U Harrison, who had studied at Bedford College, London, was appointed as from 1 September 1889. In reporting her appointment at the Prize Giving in August of that year the Reverend H Smith referred to her as 'a lady in every sense of the word' and 'an enthusiast in education'. Certainly under her guidance for the next thirty years the school continued to grow and develop. The pupil roll steadily increased, new buildings were added and equipped and the curriculum was broadened.

Initially she was to receive a salary of £80 per year as well as capitation fees of £1 for every boarder above ten and 10s for each day pupil above 25. One interesting condition of her appointment was that she had to agree that if she left her post she would not set up or teach in another school within thirty miles of King's Lynn. There was clearly a fear in those days that a head mistress who left would attract pupils from her old school to her new one. As well as Miss Harrison, the revised Prospectus listed three new resident mistresses, Miss Moffett BA, Miss Bartlett and Mlle Sirot, in addition to two of those who had worked under Miss Bannister (Miss Mead and Miss Bold). There was also a visiting mistress, Miss W Clifford-Smith. Since Miss Harrison was not a graduate it was felt that the Second Mistress should be one and so Miss Moffett was appointed from September 1889. However she did not prove satisfactory and was asked to leave at the end of the term. Over the coming years there was a fairly high turnover of staff, in some cases because Miss Harrison was not happy with their performance.

Soon after her arrival, in a letter to parents, Miss Harrison said that her aim would be 'to develop in every possible way the best powers of each individual scholar by trying to cultivate in her a genuine love for learning and for all that is courteous, refined and womanly.' There was no doubt in her mind that education was not simply about acquiring knowledge and information but about developing the whole person.

She brought in a much more relaxed atmosphere than had been the norm under her predecessor. Many years later Miss Ethel Waldegrave, former pupil and teacher at the school, recalled that Miss Harrison had at once instituted playtime and dancing on the landings. This was confirmed by Mabel Howell, also quoted in Chapter 1:

> 'With Miss Harrison's coming many changes were made and the very severe discipline was much relaxed….We were now allowed to dance on the middle landing during the morning break and later on to use swings in the loft over Dr Plowright's stables. In this loft for a very short time we were drilled by Sgt. Lorrimer, an ex-army man, who drilled the boys of the private and elementary schools of the town. Soon, however, Miss Glasier came to the school and taught calisthenics and we wore proper gym dresses and had the usual paraphernalia of barbells, Indian clubs etc. and now we learned to walk as ladies should!'

One of Miss Harrison's first initiatives was to open a kindergarten, in January 1890. It had an elementary class for children aged three to five and an intermediate class for five to seven year olds and both boys and girls were admitted. A certificated kindergarten teacher was employed.

It did not make a profit in the early years because numbers were low but it was seen by the Head Mistress as important as it provided a sound basis for the main school. The kindergarten was to be an important feature of the school until 1948 when the provisions of the 1944 Education Act came into force and the charging of fees was banned. One of the other two forms in the preparatory department was closed in 1950 and one survived until 1952. Many local gentlemen have got some amusement by telling new acquaintances that they went to the Girls' High School.

Near the beginning of her time as Head, perhaps in an effort to get things done, she went beyond what the Chairman saw as her responsibilities. In November 1890 the Reverend H Smith issued a memorandum in which he stated that the Head Mistress should approach him rather than other Directors of the company when decisions had to be made.

'In the daily and hourly management of the school very much must necessarily and rightly be left to the discretion of the Head mistress. With a school however so large as the High School, which shows signs of still further increase, cases not infrequently arise, the decision of which involves considerable responsibility. It has been her practice hitherto to go to the homes or places of business of such Directors as seemed most accessible in search of this advice. This appears to be a most unseemly position in which to place a Head Mistress, and it has the further disadvantage of occasioning a considerable waste of time. Besides it is quite possible that a Head Mistress might be careful to seek out those Directors whom she supposed most favourable to her own preconceived view.'

This can certainly be seen as a rather public rebuke. In order to establish clear areas of responsibility he devised a set of Rules for the Management of the School – nineteen in all - which were adopted in December 1890. The role of the Head Mistress was clearly defined and the pre-eminent position of the Chairman stressed. This was one of a small number of signs of disagreement in Miss Harrison's thirty years as Head Mistress but, as we shall see below, the Governors bent over backwards to keep her when there was the possibility of her resigning. A most curious entry in the Directors' Minutes in August of 1892 reads as follows:

'Agreed that it be represented to the Head Mistress that some of the Directors were of the opinion that it was advisable in the interests of the School that gentlemen should not be invited to parties at the School House.'

One wonders what had been going on! When in December 1893 Miss Harrison asked if she could attend their meetings, the Directors agreed only that she might attend 'part of the meetings by invitation'. In a further sign that the Directors found that she occasionally exceeded her authority Miss Harrison was reminded in 1904 that she should submit the names of staff to the Governors for approval *before* they were appointed. And in April 1906 in the following minute the Head Mistress is taken to task:

'Read a letter from the Head Mistress stating that she had paid £40 for additional help. Resolved that the Governors do not see their way to repay any part of the amount at present and insist that in future Miss Harrison will not incur such liabilities.'

From the very early years, as already indicated in Chapter 1, the annual Prize Giving became an important opportunity for the school to demonstrate its success. The normal pattern was to have a concert and one or more short plays as well as the distribution of prizes. Reports would be given by the Chairman, the Head Mistress and external examiners, and a distinguished guest would make a short speech and present the prizes. Detailed accounts of the proceedings were carried in the local press. An interesting feature of Miss Harrison's first Prize Giving, held at the Music Hall (also known as the Athenaeum) in July 1890, was that it started, as one would expect, with the National Anthem but, in honour of the Princess of Wales, concluded with the Danish National Anthem, the words of which were printed in the programme. The occasion became a major event on the calendar. In 1892 some 800 guests attended as well as 200 pupils and staff. These included not only parents and other townspeople but also many of the clergy and gentry from the surrounding areas.

It is in Prize Giving speeches that we glean an insight into some of the prevailing views of the day. In 1894, for example, in reference to the report of the external examiners on the work of the girls in needlework, the Chairman said:

'It is gratifying to find that in the opinion of the three lady experts in the gentle and feminine art of needlework, the sewing of the girls is so excellent. For my part I should be very sorry if needlework were at all neglected in the school. The future sphere of many girls will be domestic, wielding the needle more frequently than the pen; and it is of the last importance that they should be fitted for their future by a thorough knowledge of darning, patching, cutting out and making garments.'

Fortunately attitudes towards the education of girls have radically changed since those days and today girls out-perform boys in many public examinations.

In 1895 a major change took place in the status of the school. It was decided by the Directors that the Company should be wound up and a new non-profit-making association formed. The school would be incorporated as a public school like the Lynn Grammar School, making it possible for it to benefit from an annual grant of over £100 from the County Council. Schools were not eligible for these grants if a dividend was paid to shareholders as had been the case since 1887. In order to make the change it was necessary to raise £390, the value of the shares in the existing company. Many of the Directors agreed to forfeit all or part of the money they had invested, to the value of £190. The remaining £200 was eventually raised by subscription following an appeal to local people. In September 1895 the new instrument of government entitled *Memorandum and Articles of Association of the Incorporated King's Lynn High School for Girls* was published. The School would be run by a board of eleven governors, nine elected by members of the Association and two by Norfolk County Council. The Reverend H Smith remained the Chairman.

In 1898 other alterations were made whereby the number of governors was increased to thirteen, six to be appointed by the Association and seven by Norfolk County Council. This ensured major support from the County Council for the proposals to expand the school's premises.

A further change in the status of the school took place in November 1908 when a Public Trust was created and the name was changed to the *West Norfolk and King's Lynn High School for*

Girls. There were to be fifteen governors, including twelve representative governors: one appointed by the Queen, eight by Norfolk County Council (at least two of whom would be women), two by King's Lynn Town Council and one by the University of Cambridge. The other three would be co-optative governors, one of whom would be a woman.

Numbers on roll rose steadily in the first ten years from 49 in 1887 to 138 in 1897. Although most pupils were fee paying, after 1895, 25% of the places for girls in the main school had to go to those awarded county scholarships. This was one of the conditions of the county council grant. Another condition was that the kindergarten had to be self financing. After 1897, although the number of boarders remained steady at about 20, the overall total fell, albeit unevenly, to a low of 107 in 1909-10. In 1904 a report from a committee of the Governors looking into the school's finances suggested that since the admission of a large number of county scholars the numbers of other day pupils had fallen off. However after 1909-10 there was a steady increase. Numbers were up to 144 two years later, and to 171 just before World War 1. At the beginning of the War numbers on roll were up to 213 and a year later, with a record intake of 57 pupils, there were 235. In 1918-19 there were 311 on roll, of whom 17 were boys in the kindergarten.

One reason for the increase in numbers after 1909-10 was that from September 1906 the school had become a Pupil Teacher Centre. In the records is a copy, dated 1911, of the County scheme to send children at age 14, the leaving age in elementary schools at that time, to secondary schools such as the Girls' High School. Maintenance grants to cover the costs of tuition, railway expenses and the cost of a mid-day meal, were available up to age 17, at which point they could be placed in an elementary school for a year and receive a salary of £15. Alternatively they could stay at the secondary school and continue to receive the grant but no salary. In 1912 the High School had fifteen pupil teachers. The Grammar School in contrast had only two. In a letter to the head teachers of local elementary schools in 1913, Miss Harrison asked for the names of girls who could be personally recommended as suitable candidates for the teaching profession – 'suitable in character, physique, voice and abilities to take up teaching as their life work'. They would sit an examination and 'a few girls of 14' would be selected for the maintenance scholarships. The education at the High School would include practical training in an elementary school and qualify the girls to become un-certificated teachers if they passed the necessary examinations.

As numbers increased it was necessary to look at the provision of additional accommodation. However it was also as a result of a threat by Miss Harrison that action was taken in May 1891 to lease a large house in King Street next to Ferry Lane as a boarding house. In April of that year Miss Harrison had written a letter of resignation to the Governors in which she said she was finding the growing responsibility of so large a day school together with a boarding house more than she could bear. This was despite the fact that in January 1890 Miss Bold's salary had been increased in recognition of the fact that she assisted the Head Mistress in superintending the house. Miss Harrison said that she would be willing to stay if the two were entirely separate and if she could have rooms and a servant in the Day School. The Governors obviously decided to accede to her request. They also appointed a Matron for the boarding house.

The new property was described as having a pleasant garden, with lawns for three tennis courts, extending down to the river. In 1897 the owner of the boarding house, Miss Garrard, died and together with an adjoining property it was put up for sale. Both were bought by the Governors for £2126 with the help of a grant of £1000 from the County Council. A bank loan was taken out for £985, leaving £141 outstanding.

In November 1898 Miss Harrison again indicated that she would resign the following Easter because of ill health. However the Governors asked her to reconsider and offered to 'do anything to relieve her of as much strain as possible'. By March the following year the Chairman reported that she was in much better health and had withdrawn her resignation. She submitted a detailed report containing a number of suggestions which included the provision of a gymnasium.

In August 1899 the Governors discussed the building of a hall behind the boarding house. An architect was engaged to draw up plans and it was decided that an appeal should be made to raise the estimated £500 that would be needed. However the following year it was realised that a much more ambitious plan was necessary. New owners had acquired the Trenowath Building and initially gave the school notice to quit at Michaelmas 1900. After negotiations it was agreed that the school would continue to lease the building up to 1903 at £80 per year and put in place plans to build new classrooms, laboratories and other school buildings at the rear of the boarding house.

On 10 July 1901 a Mayoral Reception was held with the aim of raising the money needed for the new buildings. Several hundred people came and were entertained by music and given refreshments. A number of guest speakers, including the Bishop of Hertford, sometime Headmaster of Rugby School, spoke in aid of the appeal for funds. The Reverend H Smith, Chairman of Governors, explained the situation which had necessitated the appeal. He said that the Governors had been given the option to buy the Trenowath Rooms for £2000 but he felt that this would 'only be a makeshift' arrangement since 'no house not built for the purpose' was 'really suitable for such a large school as ours.' In fact he said that the school's external examiners had 'expressed astonishment that so much good work could be done in a building so little adapted for the work of a large school.' To put up a purpose-built school on the land already owned by the Association was the obvious solution. The cost was estimated at £2500 and it was hoped that the people of King's Lynn and district would support the project. As it turned out, and as is often the case, it was to cost considerably more than the original estimate.

The subscription list published shortly after the Mayoral Reception was headed by the King and Queen who donated fifty guineas and twenty-five guineas respectively. Where royalty leads others follow. Major contributors included Mr Lee Warner, the Chairman of Norfolk County Council Technical Education Committee, and Mr Alfred Jermyn who each gave £100. Mr W J Lancaster, who would within a few years pay for a new Boys' Grammar School to be built on the Gaywood Road, promised £50. Even staff at the school made modest contributions to the fund, for example Miss Bold, the Drawing and Music Mistress, gave two guineas. Over £730 had been promised within days of the Mayoral Reception and by April 1902 the fund had reached £2425, including a grant from the County Council. In order to help raise the further amount still needed, a Bazaar, with refreshment stalls, tournaments, plays and musical entertainments, was held on three successive days in April. The Bazaar was opened by the Countess of Leicester and raised a further £364. In the end the new buildings cost £3514. Of this Norfolk County Council had paid £1650, £1682 had been raised by subscriptions and the Bazaar, leaving £182 still outstanding in 1904.

The new building came into use in January of 1903. It was described in the press as 'an unpretentious but substantial and commodious block, some 160 feet in length running parallel with and adjoining Ferry Lane….constructed of red brick, having roofs covered with French tiles, and adjoining at their eastern extremity the boarding house, a portion of which has been slightly modified in order to effect a convenient junction.' The hall is described as a lofty room,

The school decorated for the visit of the Princess of Wales in October 1904

An invitation to the 1904 Prize Giving

Distribution of Prizes by H.R.H. the Princess of Wales and Presentation of Purses for Building Fund.

West Norfolk and Lynn High School

The Chairman and Governors request the pleasure of the Company of

Mr. & Mrs. Harbage

On Wednesday, the 19th October, 1904, at 3.30, at the High School, King Street, King's Lynn.

All Seats will be reserved, the price being 5/- each.

Purses for Presentation to Her Royal Highness should be of not less than Five Guineas, or Three Guineas from children under 16.

An early answer stating number of Seats required and accompanied by remittance for tickets, should be sent to the Secretary, Mr. Anderson, High School, King's Lynn.

Promises of Purses will also be gratefully received.

54 feet long by 25 feet wide. 'It is evidently intended to be useful rather than ornamental, but there is nothing unsightly'. On the north side of the hall, and running the full length of the building, was a wide corridor with a flat zinc-covered roof. From this there was access to five classrooms, one slightly smaller than the others, on the ground floor beyond the hall and to a staircase which led to the upper floor, on which was another classroom of similar size to those below, and two much larger rooms, an art studio and a science laboratory, although the latter at that stage was still unequipped.

It was hoped that a member of the Royal Family would perform an official opening of the new building. For whatever reason this did not occur but on 19 October 1904 the Princess of Wales, later Queen Mary, was the principal guest at Prize Giving. After presenting the prizes she accepted donations of money in white satin purses with the aim of clearing the debt on the purchase of the school house and the building work. The invitations to the event had informed guests that there would be a charge of 5s for reserved seats and if they intended to make a presentation to the Princess the purses were to contain not less than five guineas, or three guineas in the case of children under 16 years. In all some 29 purses were presented. After the entertainment, which included scenes from *Alfred the Great,* a play for children, and extracts from *Perseus,* dramatised from Charles Kingsley's *Heroes,* the Princess toured the school and took tea before leaving by motor car for Sandringham.

The 1902 building from the upper garden

By 1909 there was again an accommodation problem. The building used from January 1903 had been intended for 140 pupils but that number had already been exceeded and Board of Education Inspectors had said the existing accommodation was only adequate for 100 pupils. A small house opposite the school had been hired at £18 per quarter for use in the case of sickness among the boarders and because the number of boarders had increased a number of the teachers were living off the school premises. In 1911 a grant of £2000 was agreed by Norfolk County Council to build four new classrooms, a drying room and cloakrooms. This would provide accommodation for 80 pupils making the total capacity 180 and it was hoped that this would be adequate to cope with numbers over the following twenty years. The new extension was officially opened by Mrs Hamon Le Strange on 27 June 1912. Mrs Le Strange was presented with a silver-gilt key with an enamelled shield, on one side of which was the Le Strange arms and on the other the arms of Lynn. The photographs show the building in about 1912.

Mrs Hamon Le Strange at the Official Opening of the 1912 extension

How successful was the school in the period up to the end of the First World War? As mentioned in Chapter 1, in the early years of the High School, the girls were entered for examinations set by a number of different bodies. For the period of five years from 1891-92 to 1895-96 the total number of successes was 366. This included 225 passes from the South Kensington School of Art, 42 from the College of Preceptors and 36 in Music from the Royal Academy, the Royal College of Music and Trinity College of Music. In the Cambridge Locals there were 11 Senior, 31 Junior and 7 Preliminary passes. It was the Cambridge Locals which were to become the main examinations taken by the girls at the High School until just after World War 1, although

The 1912 building from the lower garden

Drill in the playground about 1912.

many continued to be entered for other examinations in Art and Music well into the twentieth century. Results in the Locals were graded into first, second and third class honours and pass levels. Distinctions were also awarded in individual subjects. The following table, taken from the 1904 Prospectus gives a summary of information for the period from 1893 to 1903:

Successes in Public Examinations, December 1893 to December 1903.

London Matriculation	(1st Division - 9; 2nd Division – 3)	12
Senior Cambridge Locals	Honours (1st Class – 1; 2nd Class – 7; 3rd Class – 11)	19
	Passes	18
	(Subject distinctions - 18)	
Junior Cambridge Locals	Honours (1st Class – 10; 2nd Class – 8; 3rd Class – 14)	32
	Passes	99
	(Subject distinctions - 49)	
Board of Education (Art)	Advanced (1st Class – 51; 2nd Class 61)	112
	Elementary (1st Class 103; 2nd Class 246)	349

In the Cambridge Locals at both Junior and Senior levels the examination included a preliminary section and a separate subject section. In the Juniors, for example, the preliminary examination included reading aloud, writing from dictation, English grammar and arithmetic. Students also had to satisfy the examiners in at least two subjects (taken from religious knowledge, English, Latin or Greek, French or German, mathematics, natural philosophy and zoology or botany). In the Seniors they had to pass in three subjects in Part ll of the examination, (selected from religious knowledge, history, Latin and Greek, French and German, mathematics, physical science, zoology and botany, drawing and music.) In both examinations religious knowledge was compulsory unless parents objected. Students normally had to be under 16 years to take the Junior and under 18 to take the Senior examinations.

There were some outstanding student achievements in the early years of the school. In 1895 four students passed the University of London Matriculation examination. Mahetabel Teare, Florence Swann, Margaret Smith and Ethel Curtis (from left to right in the photograph overleaf) not only passed but passed well in what, according to Miss Harrison, was a difficult test and had become the first girls from the High School to attain 'the right to wear the cap and gown of an undergraduate of London University.' Ethel Curtis had also gained first place in the Senior County Scholarship examination in 1894 and Florence Swann was in fourth place.

Two of the girls who matriculated in 1895 went on to gain degrees. In 1900 Miss Harrison reported that one of them, Ethel Curtis, together with another High School girl, Mabel Copley, had graduated the previous year from London University. 'They are our first B.A.s and I suppose the first girl graduates from King's Lynn.' The number of students entering university in these early years was inevitably low but a trend had been set. By 1904 the school could boast eight graduates:

Students who graduated 1893 to 1904

Beatrice Green	MA (London)
Ethel Curtis	BA (London)
Mabel Copley	BA (London)
Florence Swann	BA (London)
Agnes Green	BA (London)
Olive Johnson	BA (Wales)
Winifred Linnell	BSc (London)
Maud Sturton	Mental and Moral Science Tripos (Cantab)

Maud Sturton could not at that stage be listed as having a degree, since it was not until 1920 at Oxford and 1921 at Cambridge that women were awarded degrees, although they could sit the university examination papers.

Another landmark was passed in 1906 when Ethel Hovel gained an Open Exhibition to Bedford College in London.

In 1910 Dorothy Chadwick was placed first among all the 1015 girls entered for the Board of Education Art Examination, which had replaced that offered by South Kensington College of Art. However, as mentioned above, the Cambridge Locals became the main examinations taken in the period up to the end of World War 1. In 1914 there were 24 Senior passes and 14 Junior passes. Hilda Catton was awarded 1st Class Honours at the Senior level, gained distinctions in both English and mathematics and in the latter came second out of the 1605 girls entered. In the previous year Mary Cross had been awarded 1st Class Honours in the Junior Locals and came second out of all 3459 candidates in History and third out of 3412 in French.

Despite her assertion in 1900 that the first two girls from

Four students who passed the London University matriculation examination in 1895.

Mary Cross (centre) and her form in 1914-15

Lynn had graduated, at the 1915 Prize Giving, Miss Harrison reported that Nora Parsons was the first girl to gain a BA Degree who had been 'entirely educated' at the High School, presumably from the kindergarten through to the sixth form. She also mentioned some spectacular sets of results in the Cambridge Locals. Following her success at the Junior level, Mary Cross passed the Senior Locals with 1st Class honours and five distinctions, reported by Miss Harrison to be the best results of any girl in the UK. She was a awarded a Senior County Scholarship worth £65 per year for three years and gained a place at Bedford College, London. In addition Mary was awarded the Queen's Prize for Good Conduct in 1916*. The 1914-15 photograph shows Mary Cross in the centre of the group. The dates of the other two photographs are unknown but are from the same period.

In the Junior Locals in 1915 two girls, who had previously been pupils at St James Girls' School, Irene Beckett and Hilda Francis, were both awarded 1st Class Honours with distinctions in the same five subjects. Many years later Irene Beckett (1911-19) and a member of staff for two years after leaving school recalled her pleasure at receiving Miss Harrison's congratulations written on headed notepaper. She said that her use of the words 'brilliant' and 'magnificent' compensated for all the cramming. However Irene remembered becoming distraught when it was announced that the girls were to wear gym tunics that year at Prize Giving rather than white dresses, as she and Hilda had been bought lovely new dresses in readiness for receiving their prizes. Fortunately the 'sympathetic Head' kindly let them wear them and 'we must have looked like May Queens amid all the sober navy blue.' As a result of their examinations the two girls were awarded County Intermediate Scholarships worth £30 per year for two years. They both went on to gain 1st Class Honours and distinctions in the Senior examinations two years later but received no prizes as none were awarded later in the War.

* 60 years later her granddaughter Susan Cross would also win the Queen's Prize.

Form VB in about 1916

Miss Bowling and her form in about 1917

Reports by Inspectors for the Board of Education provided independent assessments on the success or otherwise of schools. Inspections at the High School took place in both 1909 and 1914. No written copy of the first exists but the Governors received an oral report which stressed the need for the following: more classrooms, better desks and some black boards and easels; the provision of instruction in cookery; more gymnastic equipment and the provision of remedial drill; more books for the library; and the need to increase salaries to attract stronger teachers. Several of these suggestions were implemented soon afterwards, for example some salaries were increased and a drill mistress was appointed. As we have already seen, additional buildings were provided in 1912.

The 1914 Board of Education Report refers to the steady increase in numbers of day pupils since the previous inspection, from 118 to 171, much of it due to the use made of the school by Norfolk County Council for the education of elementary school teachers 'in which this school is playing a very important part.' There is reference to the recent additions to the school buildings which it was accepted provided adequate teaching accommodation. However it was pointed out that lavatory and office provision were still below what was required. Equipment was said to be generally satisfactory but some further apparatus for physical training was needed.

The Headmistress was singled out for praise. 'The School owes a great debt to her wise and enthusiastic oversight and to her loyalty to its interests.' The staff was as a whole 'a fair one' and included some members who were 'quite strong teachers' and there was 'only one really weak spot.' It was pointed out that salaries in the past had not been high enough to attract or to hold well-qualified staff, especially in science.

Another criticism was that 'the corporate life of the school was not very pronounced and school societies have rather an ephemeral existence.' It was suggested that the girls were somewhat lacking in initiative and were content to accept what the staff offered rather than developing activities on their own account. This rather echoes one of the points made about the teaching, that it was in general too didactic and that staff did not encourage the girls to do enough for themselves.

The Report concluded:

'This is a very pleasant school which serves the needs of the locality admirably. The standard of work has advanced since the last Full Inspection, the improvement in staff, and its greater permanence, having its effect. A further advance would undoubtedly follow if the girls were always required to do more for themselves and less were done for them by their teachers. The tone and discipline are maintained on a high level.'

Less than a year after the inspection, in a report dated 15 March 1915, Miss Harrison made a strong case for additional teaching and boarding accommodation. She describes the teaching accommodation as excellent except for the need for a domestic science room for cookery and needlework and a reference library. At that stage the science laboratory was also used for cookery. She also pointed out that the boarding accommodation, especially the kitchen, dining room and offices were far from satisfactory. She suggested that a large house should be hired for the boarders, away from the school but not too far, and that the hostel, used only for bedrooms should be given up. If this were done then the boarding house could be used to provide the additional teaching rooms needed.

By the autumn of 1915 arrangements had been made for the boarders to transfer to a large house opened specifically for the purpose by Miss Collier as a private venture. She entered into a contractual agreement with the governors to provide suitable accommodation which would be recommended to parents. Surplus furniture from the school boarding house was to be let or sold to Miss Collier.

The boarding house was no more. Indeed the days of the boarders at the High School were numbered. In a letter to parents dated 6 August 1919 Mr G H Anderson, the Clerk to the Governors, said that Miss Collier had 'seen fit to give very short notice of her intention to terminate the arrangements….to receive boarders at Moreton House' and it was not possible to secure another house for the purpose. However another hostel for 15 girls was established at Everard House initially under Mrs W O Jones and this arrangement continued until Easter 1925. For a few years into the 1920s some girls also lived in lodgings approved by the Head Mistress but essentially it had become a day school.

What was the school like during the early years? The normal hours were from 9 to 12.15 and from 2.30 to 4 or 4.30 pm. However on occasions changes to these times were agreed. In November 1912, for example, it was decided that there would be no afternoon school for the rest of the term because of the long distances some girls had to walk in the dark from different railway stations to their homes. Lynn girls were allowed to attend school for preparation work. It is not clear if this change was made each winter but Governors' Minutes show that in October 1915 it was decided that as from 2 November to the middle of the following term the school hours would be from 9 am to 12 noon and from 1.30 to 3 pm to allow girls to get home in daylight. The following year it was decided that from 23 October until the middle of the following term the school hours would be from 9 am to 12.50 pm on six days per week, with the school open in the afternoons for preparation work.

The following school rules, introduced in 1913, were straightforward and few in number:

1   Pupils coming to and going from the High School, in trains etc. are to behave in a quiet and orderly manner.

2   It is required that plain hats should be worn, with only the school ribbon.

3   During school hours simple loose dresses should be worn, low-heeled shoes and no jewellery except brooches and watches, and hair should be neatly tied back.

4   Girls taking gymnastics or cookery lessons must have dresses, shoes and pinafores thought suitable by the Head Mistress.

5   Everything belonging to a pupil must be plainly marked.

It is perhaps strange that there is no mention of the need for good behaviour in school. It must have been taken as given. However even in those days the girls occasionally pushed the boundaries. Mabel Howell, quoted above, tells how they played up the Singing Master:

'I recall with pleasure also the singing lessons with Miss Bold and afterwards with Mr Cross, who was the organist at Sandringham. Discipline was not a very strong point with the latter and a mistress was always in attendance. There was one girl who always sang on one note only, and efforts to find her caused much fun, for always the buzz came from a place where Mr Cross was not.'

It would seem nothing changes. An almost identical story, but involving a different visiting teacher, Mr Shirley, was recalled by Peggy Howes, who was at the school over a decade after Mabel Howell:

'The Singing Master, whose full initials, by the way, were ASS was known amongst us as 'the Professor'. He visited us on Friday mornings, and as we awaited his arrival at the top of the hall, we speculated on his latest choice of wearing apparel – purple socks and green striped tie, or a red and yellow spotted tie, with blue socks.

'Good morning! Ladies, we will have a new song this morning. I'll just let you know how it goes', and seating himself at the piano, with his back more or less to us, he began his performance. What were we doing in the mean time? Listening? The previous day's dancing classes had been held in the hall, and the beautifully polished floor gave us an opportunity not to be missed….The music stopped. 'Ladies! Ladies!' Very innocently we regained our former positions and singing began. But where was that discordant voice? Always at the furthest point from the Professor as he prowled round. Alas! Our gleeful singing lessons could not last. To our utter dismay we were always faced by a grim-looking Senior English Mistress who stayed throughout until the end of the term. Ah well we had fun!'

Rather more serious breaches of discipline obviously did occur on occasions, for example in February 1918. Complaints had been received about poor behaviour on the train and after investigations had taken place three culprits were identified and admonished by Miss Harrison. Shortly afterwards it seems that one of the girls re-offended and the girl's parents were informed that their daughter could not be allowed to continue as a pupil at the school.

In 1898 Miss Harrison was assisted by eleven resident mistresses and five visiting teachers. Only two of them at that stage had degrees. The number of teachers in 1909 was similar, although by that date six had degrees or the equivalent. Miss W B Jones was listed as having passed the Cambridge Modern Languages Tripos. There were in addition three student mistresses. The salaries at this stage were not high. Miss Harrison received £100 per year plus a capitation allowance of £1 per pupil. That gave her a total of £259 13s 4d in 1908. The other mistresses were paid between £50 and £80 depending on length of service. However in 1913 the Governors adopted two salary scales - in Class 1 the maximum was £150 and in Class 2 it was £120. There were increments of £5 per year for those appointed below the maximum. These were salaries for mistresses who were resident and £40 was deemed to be included for board and lodging. An undated prospectus for about 1916 lists thirteen assistant mistresses, and again six of them had degrees or the equivalent. Miss Bradshaw is described as having passed the Oxford Final Honours examination in French.

The records show two early examples of co-operation with the King Edward VII Grammar School. In February 1910 the Governors approved the formation of a French conversation class jointly with the boys and in October 1912 it was decided that holidays would be arranged so as to coincide with the Grammar School. There was also community use of the school premises in these early days, for example in March 1916 the use of the hall for a public lecture by the Dean of Norwich, in connection with the Shakespeare Tri-centenary, was approved for a fee of 10s. Ambulance lectures on the other hand took place free of any charge. Perhaps the most startling example comes from July of 1917 when it was agreed that volunteers could use the lawn for machine-gun practice on three evenings a week. Presumably term had ended!

Memories of teachers from the period up to 1919 (and indeed for later years) are provided by a number of former pupils in articles written in 1962 for an anniversary edition of the School Magazine, from which the story by Peggy Howes above was reproduced.

The Head Mistress, Miss Harrison, was highly regarded by both staff and pupils. Peggy Howes said that she was held in 'great reverence and awe' but she was 'very humanly understanding and loved by all'. Hilda Bremner (1900-1910) at 70 still had great affection for the school. She particularly mentioned Miss Harrison's ability to make pupils love English Literature:

'I can still feel the thrill at a mental picture of her bursting into the classroom (the mistress of which was perhaps ill), a pile of books containing some play unknown to us in her arms and the joy with which we were simultaneously reading and acting the play within a very few minutes. There was no sitting down to 'learn by heart' and yet even now I can recite poems learnt only by hearing them read and then reading them in one of these classes, taken all too rarely by the head.'

Peggy Ellison, the 1923 Queen's Prize winner, remembered sitting nervously in a big room, used for Governors' Meetings, waiting to see the Head Mistress about admission to the school but 'the charm and vivacity of Miss Harrison dispelled all fears'. She recalled that Miss Harrison was always trying to think up some treat for the girls. At the end of one term when the mistresses were marking examination papers, large boxes of dressing up clothes were brought out and the older girls were instructed to do charades to amuse the younger ones.

Miss Waldegrave commented on Miss Harrison's fondness for giving the boarders small treats, such as hot sausages and special cakes for high tea on Saturdays and occasionally letting them sleep in the Summer House. They had dancing and acting every Saturday evening and always seemed happy and busy. Before 11 King Street was given up 'the boarders made the very short distance to the school walking in a crocodile and wearing hats, coats and gloves.' Did they skip along or did they walk sedately one wonders?

That Miss Harrison knew each girl as an individual is illustrated by a letter to a parent in 1913. The language however is certainly redolent of the period and reads most strangely today:

The High School
King's Lynn
1 Jan 1913

Dear Mrs Leeder

It is delightful to be able to send two such good reports.

Doris has done splendidly and won all hearts. She is the sweetest little maiden. I only hope she won't get spoilt with petting.

Grace has been most sensible and wise as elder sister and both are two of the most satisfactory pupils in the school.

With good New Year wishes

Yours very truly

Edith Harrison

A slightly less favourable view of Miss Harrison and of some of the girls at the school is found in the diary of Evelyn Pull, later Mrs Lewton Brain, mother of Diana Lewton Brain, who was

Head of French from 1963 to 1967:

'When I was thirteen I went to the King's Lynn High School and was very excited about it, going up by train every day [from Heacham] with a season ticket which I was terrified of losing. Harold [her brother] started at the Grammar School there the next term having won a scholarship. We travelled up with various boys and girls, the boys in school caps and blazers, but we wore our ordinary clothes....At the High School I was very unhappy the first term and was much ragged by the girls in the breaks and dinner hour because my father was a butcher and being very shy I suffered terribly. However some of the lessons were very enjoyable and I specialised in music....

The Headmistress was an imposing figure who swept about the school in a frock with a long train. I always felt at a disadvantage with her; she said I was so dreamy! She loved the richer ones of her pupils and the other girls laughed about how she fussed them up....'

As is often the case pupils' memories of teachers are not identical. Hilda Bremner's memories of Miss Pearson, the Mathematics teacher, were not so happy as those she had of Miss Harrison, although she claimed that in retrospect she could even enjoy the sound of her impatient voice telling her to 'take it for granted child, take it for granted' when asked to explain something.

Edith Turner (1911-17) on the other hand remembered Miss Pearson as 'that wonderful teacher of Scripture and Mathematics....Her teaching and that in English first of Miss Cleaver and later Miss Fowlds, whose tragic death in a railway accident on the Continent was such a great loss.... are the highlights of my scholastic memories.' Irene Beckett cited above, was one of four sisters who went to the High School. She too remembered fondly Miss Cleaver who 'imbued us with a love of Shakespeare' and Miss Fowlds who 'later fostered a love of his plays' and she very much enjoyed the annual visits to the theatre in Stratford. At the Governors' Meeting in December 1917 Miss Fowlds was congratulated on her excellent results in English and Composition in the Cambridge Senior Locals, a rare accolade.

Information about extra-curricular activities is sparse until 1923 when the first School Magazine was published. However in 1912 it was reported that 45 girls had joined the hockey club and that the 1st and 2nd teams had so far won all their matches. A company of girl guides had also been formed. As already mentioned the annual Prize Giving always included a programme of music and drama performed by the pupils and sometimes the staff. In 1913 Irene Beckett was Tennyson's *Oenone*, in a long white robe with golden braid. Miss Cleaver fed her 'dainty cress sandwiches' in her lodgings and helped her to learn her lines.

Also in 1913 Miss Harrison sent out an invitation to a meeting at which it was hoped that an Old Girls' Association would be formed. However it did not really get off the ground until after the War.

The 1914 Prize Giving held in December, only months after the outbreak of war, was a decidedly low key event compared with what had become the norm. It was announced that it had been decided not to hold such an elaborate programme as in past years. The girls had been employed in knitting things for the troops instead of getting up the usual musical programme. Perhaps the highlight of the event was the presentation to Miss Harrison of a gold watch and a copy of *The Rubaiyat of Omar Khayyam* to mark her twenty-five years as Head Mistress.

We have little information on the war years. However the effects were clearly felt. As from January 1915 the boarding fee was raised by £2 per term 'during the continuance of the War' because of the greatly increased prices of food, coal and all household goods. Several increases in the cost of meat were reported to the Governors, for example to 10d per pound in March 1915, to 11d in June later that year and then to 1s.1d in May 1916. In November 1915 Miss Harrison told the Governors that 37 day girls were bringing their own food to eat at lunchtime and it was decided that a nominal charge of 2s 6d per term would be charged to cover 'the use of crockery, service etc.' On a more positive side, regular collections were made in school for various war relief funds such as the Red Cross, for example between May and December of 1915, £23 11s was collected and sent off. This was a clear attempt on behalf of the school to develop the girls' social conscience. There were also cases of Belgian refugees being admitted to the school.

One thing that did change, perhaps because of the discontinuation of Prize Giving during the later part of the War and for several years afterwards, was the presentation of the Queen's Prize. Previously it had been presented at Prize Giving by the guest speaker but 1915 saw the last such event until 1923. Showing great initiative, Edith Turner, who was Head Girl in 1916-17, wrote on behalf of the school to the Hon. Mrs A R Grant, the wife of the Rector of Sandringham, and the Queen's representative on the Governing Body, to ask if Queen Alexandra would agree to present her prize in person at Sandringham instead of it being given with all the other prizes at the Annual Prize Giving. This was agreed and so the tradition was established. Edith, according to her account, was presented with a gold brooch by the Queen in 1917 at Snettisham School before going up to Bedford College in London but, because of an omission, did not receive her prize until 1921. More will be said about the first presentation at Sandringham in the next chapter.

The Art Room

Miss Clara Bold

In 1919 two very long serving members of staff retired, Miss Harrison and Miss Bold. Miss Harrison's praises have already been sung. Clara Bold had spent 32 years at the school as a teacher of art and, in the early years, music. Large numbers of girls were successful in the South Kensington and other art examinations as a result of her teaching. The photograph shows the Art Room during her time at the school. When she died in 1936 after a very short illness, warm tributes were paid by former pupils and colleagues. Miss Waldegrave, who had herself retired a year earlier, referred to her strong Irish sense of humour, her raciness of speech, her high ideals of conduct and work and her steadiness and equability in facing crises. She said that these attributes produced a personality that made a strong impression on the young. 'Her discipline might be considered severe in these days but it was tempered by such humour and geniality that it gained for her both the respect and the affection of the pupils.' Mrs Dorer, who only joined the staff in 1918, but had been a pupil in the school, remembered her 'tall upright figure in the quiet dress with the touch of magnificence afforded by the long gold chain worn outside the high collar and reaching to the waistband.' However she said that her dignity did not hold her aloof. 'She had a kind word, even a joke for us, in and out of lessons; and when she taught it was as a kind friend revealing the treasures of knowledge and accomplishment.' Mr G H Anderson, as Clerk to the Governors (and before that to the Board of Directors) had been associated with the school from the very beginning. He recalled that in the trying early years of the school Miss Bold's tact and sound judgement were most valuable in dealing with many of the problems of school life. She had never confined herself to her teaching duties but had been ready to help with anything.

She and Miss Harrison developed a strong friendship over the many years that they worked together and from 1923 they shared a home. When Miss Bold went blind, she was very fortunate to have her friend to look after her and when she died in 1936 Miss Harrison wrote a charming letter to the Old Girls which was reproduced in the School Magazine:

Dear Girls,

Your kind Miss Bold died after only two days' illness, last March. She had absolutely no pain, and passed away gently in her sleep.

Though blind, she has been very happy in her beautiful garden. It has a lovely lawn, pleasant summer-houses, apple trees, roses and hedges of lavender.

Every day, summer and winter, she never forgot to feed 'my dear little birds,' who quite knew her.

I think some of you would like a portrait of her: if so will you send me your address?

Your affectionate old Head Mistress,

Edith Harrison

5 Stephen Street,
Rugby

So we have a photograph of Miss Bold but unfortunately not one of Miss Harrison.

Clearly many recall their time at the school up to and including the First World War as a happy period in their lives. Miss Harrison retired in 1919 after thirty successful years as Head Mistress at the school and her contribution to its development in these formative years was considerable. In August 1919 she was presented with an oak bureau by the Governors and Clerk 'as a small appreciation of her work....' She lived to a grand old age and from her retirement home in Hunstanton was able to keep in touch with the school. Her death, on 4 August 1953 aged 95, was reported in the School Magazine and Margaret Metcalf wrote as follows:

> 'Older members of the OGA will remember her kindness and deep concern for the girls. They will remember with affection her sweeping gowns and elegant gold necklaces and above all her great dignity. To many she became a legend in her own lifetime.'

However a new era was to begin with the appointment of her successor, Miss Williamson.

3. 1919-44. Quiet, steady work and progress.

Miss Rose Williamson, who had a 1st Class Honours degree in English from London University, was appointed to be Head Mistress of the High School as from September 1919 and she stayed until 1944. There were a 101 applications for the post and, from a long list of seven, four were selected for interview including an internal candidate, Miss E M Pearson. In the event three attended for interview and Miss Williamson was appointed. Her starting salary was fixed at £350 rising by £20 per year to £450. In 1929 a new salary scale was introduced whereby the Head's salary was to be £600 from 1 April, rising by increments of £15 per year to £675.

From the start her approach was to be different in a number of ways from that of Miss Harrison. Her views were clearly expressed in 1923 in her report at the first Speech Day after WW1. She said that the desire to gather up marks in order to come out at the top of the class, or in other words, 'to have the glory of beating others', was an aspect of human nature which should not be encouraged. Good work might be done under such a stimulus but something more valuable might be lost.

This was the reason why, two years previously, she had decided to stop arranging girls in order of merit according to their marks in the term examinations. Instead there was a range of standards in which they were placed alphabetically not knowing their actual marks.
The aim was to allow pupils to compare their present with past achievements without reference to the work of others. As we shall see below she steadfastly opposed the introduction of Houses as competitive units even when suggested by HMI.

Miss Williamson and a section of the 1920 school photograph

Although Miss Williamson was against competition between individuals she evidently thought competition between groups could be beneficial. From 1929 two new prizes were awarded, one to the form which was 'most successful in cultivating gentle and quiet behaviour' and the other to the form which made its form room 'as pleasant looking as possible.' Sheila Manning (Nicholson), who now lives in Old School Court, recalls that the prizes when she was at the school were prints of *Girl with a Pearl* Earring by Vermeer and of *The Avenue at Middelharnis* by Hobbema. They were hung in the rooms of the winning forms. Miss Williamson was clearly of the view that academic success was not everything. In 1935 she stressed the importance of generosity of spirit to the audience at Speech Day, and said that the highest aim of education was 'to see girls ready to give rather than to take, to put into the pool more than they took out of it.' However, according to Sheila Manning, she was quite passionate about girls staying on into the sixth form to take the Higher School Certificate.

In Miss Williamson's first year, 1919-20, the number on roll was 345, including 19 boys and, although the numbers did rise significantly in the two following years, by 1922-23 the roll was down to 336 pupils and for the rest of the decade and into the first part of the 1930s the number remained stable at around 330. Despite the fact that there was no increase in numbers an extension to the main buildings was necessary by the end of the 1920s. As is described below this was largely because of the addition of more specialist facilities. At the end of the 1930s numbers in the school were still around 340 including about a dozen boys.

Some changes occurred in the interwar period in both the composition of the school population and in the sources of funding. In 1924 Norfolk Education Committee decided that in future years, in order to qualify for a maintenance grant, the free places in the school would have to be increased from 25% to 40%. Three years later the school ceased to receive any capitation money from the Board of Education; from 1 August 1927 grant aid was provided solely by Norfolk. In 1930 the Governors agreed to increase the free places to 50% as long as sufficient candidates passed the examination.

Numbers in the preparatory department were fairly stable during Miss Williamson's time at the school although soon after she arrived the fees had to be raised to make it financially viable. In a letter to parents in November 1920 the Clerk explained that Norfolk County Council grants to the school were conditional on the preparatory department being self-financing which it had not been hitherto. He suggested that an annual fee of 15 guineas would be required and asked if parents would confirm their willingness to pay that amount. In the event it was decided in January 1921 that the new fee would be 12 guineas per year. The kindergarten included boys as well as girls and as mentioned in Chapter 2 many local men remember their time as pupils at the High School. Geoff Bullen was there from 1927 to 1930, aged 5 to 7, before transferring to the Grammar School, and one of his most vivid memories is of the R101 airship flying above the River Great Ouse and over the High School on its way to Sandringham to be seen by George V. Geoff was in trouble when he arrived home because the airship was leaking oil and he got it all over his clothes. The end of the story was rather more serious because not long after this incident the airship crashed over France on its way to India, on 5 October 1930, with the loss of 48 lives.

Geoff Bullen was one of several generations of his family at the High School. His mother, Enid Giles, joined the school in about 1911 and her mother, Kate Bradfield, in 1889, the same year as Miss Harrison became Head Mistress. Geoff's two sisters, Barbara and Ann Bullen were also at the school as was his wife, Margaret Boulton. Many other families would be able to tell a similar tale.

The new library

During the 1920s Miss Williamson worked hard to improve the facilities. When she arrived, the only rooms for specialist teaching were the art studio and the science-cum-cookery laboratory. One of her first achievements was the creation in 1924 of a new reference library, made essential by the school having gained recognition for its Advanced Course in Modern Studies. This had been approved by the Board of Education in 1923 and, apart from the Lynn Grammar School which had an Advanced Course in Science, no other secondary school aided or administered by the Norfolk Education Authority had such a course. One aim of the new course was to help pupils to become independent learners, able to use books for study and to carry out a piece of work on their own. Over the next few years a considerable amount of money was spent on building up the library which, according to HMI in 1933 resulted in 'an admirable collection of books in English, History, French and Geography.'

Gradually other rooms were provided, for a fiction library and for music, and the kitchen and dining rooms were remodelled. There were major improvements in facilities for science and domestic science. By converting useless attics in the old building a domestic science room was brought into use in the spring of 1928 and by June 1931 the chemistry laboratory had been newly fitted and equipped. The following year specialist accommodation for work in biology and botany was ready. This enabled the science subjects to be taught to Higher School Certificate level.

Then in 1931 an extension to the teaching block was built to provide accommodation for some of the forms in the very crowded old house. The new building was erected at right angles to the

1912 section of the school with an archway allowing access from the playground via a flight of steps to the lawn and the river. The plans were only approved by the Board of Education after they were amended to include the archway. The extension included two classrooms on the ground floor, one for 30 pupils and one for 24, together with cloakrooms and toilets. On the first floor was another good-sized room for 30 pupils. Most of the cost, which came to some £2435, was met by the Norfolk Education Committee and the shortfall of £127 was taken from the balance in the preparatory department accounts. The new wing was opened in January 1932 by the Reverend Sir Francis ffolkes, Chairman of Governors.

The 1931-32 building from the lower garden

In the 1920s and 1930s the school continued to be used on occasions by the community. In September 1922, for example, it was agreed that the hall could be used for a Library and Museum lecture but a request for its use as a rehearsal space by the Amateur Operatic Society was turned down. In October of the same year the use of the hall for six lectures on Modern Art and National Life was approved, the expenses to be defrayed by the King's Lynn Arts and Science Society. Similar lettings were agreed in subsequent years.

The lack of its own playing field was a major problem for the High School. For many years hockey and tennis had been played in The Walks and netball on the school playground. However in the summer of 1924 a letter from the King's Lynn Football Club gave notice that it was to end the hiring of its field for hockey. Then for several seasons the Grammar School playing fields were used for girls' games, until in 1929 its own long-hoped for facility was finally in the school's possession. Two fields off Estuary Road in North Lynn, about 11 acres in area, were bought in January 1929 for the sum of £1200, toward which a grant of £1000 was made by Norfolk

Education Committee. By March two hockey pitches had been prepared and were in use, two tennis courts were almost ready and two more were in progress. By May 1931 another four tennis courts had been completed. A pavilion was also built.

How successful was the school academically during this period?

The School Certificate (SC) and Higher School Certificate (HSC) examinations were first introduced in 1918. They were soon to replace the previous Cambridge Local examinations taken by girls at the school. The changeover can be seen in 1922 and 1923. In 1922 three girls were the first to be successful in the new HSC while some 33 girls passed in the Senior Locals examination. The following year 22 girls were the first at the school to obtain the new School Certificate, two of them with distinctions in History.

The regulations varied over the thirty or so years that the examination was offered. In the HSC, by the 1940s, subjects could be taken at an advanced standard or at an ordinary standard. It was also possible to take subjects at a subsidiary level. Candidate had to take at least one main subject and not less than three subjects in all but no more than two at the advanced standard. In order to be awarded the HSC girls had to pass a General Paper and obtain at least six points in the other subjects. (An advanced pass in a subject counted for three points, an ordinary standard pass for two points and a pass in a subsidiary subject counted for one point.) Candidates also had to achieve a certain aggregate mark overall rather than just a series of isolated passes.

Unlike the GCE 'O' levels which were to be introduced in 1951, the School Certificate was not a single subject examination. In the 1940s it was necessary to pass in English language and in five other subjects, at least one of which had to be mathematics, a science or a language. In

The 1939 HSC and School Certificate candidates (LN)

37

The 1940 HSC and School Certificate candidates (LN)

addition, as in the HSC, candidates could be failed if they did not reach a certain standard in the examination as a whole.

During the 1920s and 1930s numbers achieving the two main examinations varied from year to year as one might expect. In the HSC the highest number of successful candidates was nine in 1935 but there were only two in 1933. In the School Certificate the number of pupils who were successful in the 1920s was generally below twenty but between twenty and thirty in the following decade. In 1944, Miss Williamson's last year at the school, five girls achieved the HSC and thirty-three gained the School Certificate. A detailed analysis of the results shows that of the 364 subject entries, only 15 (4%) were graded as very good, 160 (44%) were passes with credit, 112 were straight passes and 77 were fails. The highest number of passes (39) was achieved in Geography with 29 credits and 1 very good. There were 35 passes in English Language and 33 in General Science, but only 21 in Elementary Mathematics and 10 in Arithmetic.

There were many outstanding individual successes. In 1931 Emma Dorer passed the HSC with a distinction in French. She won a State Scholarship and, most prestigious of all, an

Emma Dorer

Open Exhibition to Girton College, Cambridge. The Governors were so delighted by the news that Miss Williamson was asked to grant the girls a holiday. Emma was also the winner of the Queen's Prize which was presented to her by Queen Alexandra at Sandringham in January 1932. While at Cambridge she won the Fanny Metcalf Prize in 1933; a year later she won the Mary Elizabeth Ponsonby Prize and was the only woman at Cambridge to be awarded 1st Class Honours in Part 2 of the Modern Languages Tripos.

Other girls to be awarded 1st Class Honours were Mona Gibson in English at Royal Holloway College in 1937 and Margery Jary in French at Leeds University in 1938. However they were not just successful in their academic work. Mona won the 100 yards Breast-stroke Cup at the University of London Swimming Championships whilst still at RHC and retained it the following year while taking a teacher-training qualification at Maria Grey College. And Margery was captain of the Women's Fencing Team at Leeds University which won the Northern Universities' Fencing Cup. Another successful sportswoman was Alice Collison who was awarded boating colours at Bedford College and was a member of the University of London Women's Light-weight Crew in 1938-39. Despite that commitment she gained Upper 2nd Class Honours in French.

Other successes included Norah Bremner who in 1933, while still at school, was awarded a travelling scholarship by the *Lynn News* for an essay on the work of the League of Nations. Her prize allowed her to attend the League of Nations Summer School in Geneva from 1 to 12 August. She went up to Royal Holloway College in 1935 to read English.

In the period up to World War 2 four other scholarships were won by High School girls. In 1935 Dora Leonard won an Open Exhibition, worth £20 a year for three years, to read History at Westfield College in London, having passed her HSC in 1933 with distinctions in Scripture and Geography, albeit not in History. Janet Howes was awarded a Bursary, worth £30 a year for three years, at the Froebel Institute in Roehampton in 1938; in the same year Pamela Sutherland, who came equal first in the examination, won an Open Scholarship, worth £50 a year for three years, to the Swanley Horticultural College; and in 1943 Jean Dunt won a similar scholarship to Swanley.

The number of High School girls at university in the inter-war period was never large. In 1925, for example, Alice Curson went to Westfield College, London and three others, Doris David, Marjorie Gilbert and Lorna Rennie went to Leeds University. The following year only two gained university places, Olive Youngs at Westfield College and Audrey Stratford at Bedford College. What was unusual was that Audrey went to study science. She had passed her HSC in 1925 in English and history with subsidiary French and mathematics but stayed on for a further year studying chemistry and botany in order to gain a place to study chemistry. In the event she graduated in 1930 with a 2nd class honours degree in Physiology and went on to have an academic career until she returned to Lynn towards the end of World War 2 to help run the family business because of her father's failing health. In Audrey's papers is a testimonial written by Miss Williamson in support of her application for a post as Lecturer in Physiology at Chelsea Polytechnic in 1932:

'....Throughout her career at school Miss Stratford showed decided intelligence and her conduct was thoroughly reliable. She gave evidence of her initiative and independent judgement while retaining an open mind to suggestion and criticism. She was a very pleasant pupil in every way and would be found a really loyal and helpful member of any teaching staff.'

Numbers going to university in the 1930s were similar. In 1935, for example, there were seven taking degrees at various London colleges, one at Cambridge and one at Leeds University. In addition there was a number of girls training to be teachers and nurses and for a range of other occupations. One of the university students at London in 1935 was Joan Wagstaff, the daughter of the Head Master of the Grammar School. She was studying medicine at University College London and in 1938 passed her LRCP and MRCS examinations and went on to take the MB degree later that year.

Although the numbers going to university from the High School in the 1930s was low compared with later decades, in terms of Norfolk schools it shows up well. County-wide statistics for Norfolk secondary schools on the destinations of leavers from 1930 to 1937 show that only two to seven girls went on to university in each of those years. The boys did not fair much better with figures of only three to ten.

During World War 2 the number gaining scholarships to enable them to go on to higher education was also very small – three in 1939, none in 1940, two in 1941, two in 1942, including Claudia Harding, who gained a place at Girton College, Cambridge, one in 1943, and one in 1944. One of the two students to be awarded major county scholarships in 1941 was Maud Howard who gained a place at Reading University. To help pay for her time at university her father sold the

A group of friends in 1939 including Maud Howard and Barbara Cook

family fishing boat, *The Daily Bread.* Presumably it was not possible to use it for fishing during the war and in any case Maud's father and older siblings were otherwise occupied. The photograph shows Maud (second from the left at the back) and friends, including Barbara Cook (on the extreme right) who was to become her sister-in-law. Both were scholarship girls, Maud from the North End and Barbara from West Lynn. Barbara did one year in the sixth form before training as a secretary and then joining the WRNS.

External evaluations of the success of the school were provided by Her Majesty's Inspectors of Schools. During the time that Miss Williamson was Head Mistress there were two main HMI inspections, one in 1923 and another in 1933. In 1923 the staff was described as hardworking and as a whole well qualified. However weaknesses in some subjects were identified. French, geography and science were singled out for criticism. Another point made was that the clubs and societies were not very strong, but the appearance of a School Magazine, the first edition of which had come out in the summer of 1923, was seen as a very positive step. Another criticism was that the prefects, chosen from the sixth form, had very limited responsibilities.

Although there had been no new buildings since the last inspection in 1914, the greater part of the School House had been made available for teaching, since apart from Miss Williamson, the staff were no longer resident. This meant that there were five additional classrooms, making fifteen in all. Despite the fact that the boarding house had been lost there were still some twelve girls living in the town in lodgings approved by the Head Mistress.

The HMI made various suggestions for improvement, some of which would be introduced in coming years. The library needed to be expanded, especially with the introduction of the Advanced Course on Modern Studies. In addition the school needed its own playing fields. The local football grounds were hired for use on Wednesday afternoons and Saturday mornings but this was not a satisfactory arrangement. It was also suggested that the school should provide a hot meal and drinks such as milk or cocoa, since a large number (about 95) stayed at school at lunchtime. Another suggestion was that Houses should be introduced for competitive purposes rather than the form, since girls could belong to the same House throughout their time at school. However, as we have seen, Miss Williamson was not keen on competition.

The Report concluded by saying that 'The standard of work, though still very low in some subjects, shows an advance since the last inspection, and the school fully maintains its local reputation.' Could be better then!

The second HMI Report of the inter-war period was much more positive. The inspectors congratulated the school on the improved facilities, 'namely an excellent playing field with suitable pavilion and a new wing to the main block of classrooms providing two good teaching rooms and an extra cloakroom.' The specialist rooms for art, biology, chemistry, domestic science and music also got a mention as did the 'pleasant and dignified room' which contained the library and a smaller room for the fiction library. The main criticism on the accommodation was that many of the rooms were too small. Although there were 16 classrooms in addition to the specialist rooms, the same as the number of forms, only two were suitable for a full-sized class, while four in the old residential building were what they described as 'no more than division rooms'; of the remaining ten, eight were nominally rooms for 24 and two for 20.

The Report said that the school had made steady progress under Miss Williamson, reflecting 'her ability to organise and run it with success.' She had a good knowledge of the girls and the staff.

The latter were academically well qualified and their teaching ability satisfactory, although there were some criticisms of chemistry, which was described as the weakest subject, of French and of mathematics. One general criticism was that there was insufficient oral work. It was also felt that in some subjects there was too little independent and individual work expected of the girls.

The lack of a House system was mentioned as in 1923 and the point was made that the Head Mistress regarded the competitive spirit developed by grouping into Houses as 'unnecessary and undesirable.'

In conclusion the inspectors said that the school had not changed greatly in the ten years since the previous inspection but what change there had been was 'distinctly for the better.' The progress of the girls through the school was well provided for and creditable success was achieved in public examinations.

In addition to the two main inspections there were at least two other short ones. In 1934 music was inspected and the brief report was very positive. The following conclusion would no doubt have given much pleasure to both Miss Williamson and Miss Drever:

Audrey Stratford in school uniform (mid 1920s)

> 'The work is so good all round as to call for little in the way of criticism or suggestion….A girl leaving this school has had every opportunity of forming a taste for music which should be an enduring influence on her life.'

General satisfaction was expressed following another HMI visit in 1940 and two teachers were singled out for special praise. The inspector commented on the excellent teaching of both Miss Beardsell in History and Miss Inglis in French.

Both the 1923 and 1933 HMI Reports

Audrey Stranger in summer uniform (late 1920s)

42

made the point that behaviour was good. That in 1923 said that the tone and discipline were maintained at a high level, while in 1933 it was said that 'the behaviour of the girls, both in the classroom and when they move about the school made a favourable impression.' Former students confirm that this was the case although the girls were not above minor infringements of the rules or teasing staff. Ann Bromhead (1939-45) remembers when Miss Williamson 'smiled but looked solemn' on seeing her in the High Street one Saturday, wearing her school blazer but not the compulsory panama hat, and at a later date being reprimanded by Miss Hilditch for not wearing her hat when cycling to school.

Rather more serious breaches of discipline obviously did occur on occasions. For example in June 1925 it was reported to the Governors that several girls had been absent without leave on the morning before the half-term break and as a result their parents were asked for an undertaking that there would be no repetition in future. One parent had not done so and had removed his daughter. Presumably he had been told that unless he agreed the girl would not be allowed to return.

Ann Bromhead says that the girls were mostly in awe of the teachers and were delighted if they shared a joke with them or made a slightly risqué remark. On one occasion in a mathematics lesson when emphasising that one referred to 'a pair of compasses', Miss Ince, whom Ann said could be very fierce, amused them by saying, 'You don't talk about a pair of knicker do you?' Similarly Miss Green, the Geography Mistress, made them laugh by telling them she had worn out the seat of her knickers sliding down scree slopes.

By the early 1920s the school uniform included a tunic, a green blazer with school badge and a velour hat with a band also showing the school badge, as shown in the photograph of Audrey Stratford (1919-26). The summer uniform with panama hat and a green and white dress can be seen in the photograph of Audrey Stranger who was at the school from 1925 to 1930.

As mentioned in Chapter 2 the status of the Queen's Prize Winner was greatly enhanced after World War 1. It had previously been awarded along with all the other prizes at Speech Day. With certain exceptions in the Second World War, from January 1920, the prize was awarded personally by the Queen at Sandringham. On the first occasion the recipient was Dorothy Wolstencroft, daughter of Mr J W Wolstencroft, the Town Clerk. She was accompanied by Sir Alfred Jermyn, the Chairman of Governors and the Head Mistress, Miss Williamson. Queen Alexandra presented Dorothy with a beautifully bound volume of the *Oxford Book of Victorian Verse* and asked her about her studies at Homerton College, Cambridge, and her intended career in teaching. The visitors were treated to a tour of the Royal apartments by the Queen and Princess Victoria.

When Queen Alexandra died in 1925 Queen Mary agreed to continue to award the prize. She presented prizes to both the 1924 and 1925 winners at Sandringham in January 1926. At least one of the Queen's Prize winners was to have the privilege of meeting Queen Mary twice. Josephine Hamson, daughter of a Lynn jeweller and the 1933 winner, received her prize from the Queen at Sandringham in January 1934. It was a leather-bound volume of the complete works of Shakespeare with the Queen's monogram and the school crest embossed in gold on the cover. In the conversation which ensued it emerged that Josephine had been born in China and so the Queen invited her to examine the various Chinese ornaments which adorned the room. Having last visited the school in 1904 Queen Mary is said to have expressed surprise when Miss Williamson told her that there were 350 students on roll and asked how they could fit so many girls into the school. Miss Williamson was able to point out that they had had new buildings

Queen Mary meeting High School Girls in 1938

since the Queen's last visit.

Josephine Hamson studied at Queen Mary College in London from which she was awarded a degree in science in 1937. The following May the Queen, on a visit to open a new hall of residence at QMC, asked to meet the three girls from Lynn who were students there. Josephine Hamson, by then taking a course in teacher training at the London Institute of Education, was able to introduce Dulcie Petts and Joan Reynolds to Her Majesty. In the photograph Josephine is facing the camera. According to the newspapers which reported the event, Queen Mary asked to be given an ordinary key to perform the opening ceremony as she already had four hundred gold and silver keys!

Josephine's links with the High School did not end in 1934. For a few years during the late 1950s, by then Mrs Tooke, she was a part-time teacher of science at the school and then in 1986 she and her husband moved into a flat, one of thirty in the newly-converted Old School Court, the former school buildings in King's Street. In fact she chose a flat in what had been the chemistry laboratory in which she had taught some thirty years earlier.

Although Queen Mary did not die until 1953 it was decided in 1937, the year after George VI ascended the throne, that henceforth the Queen's Prize would be awarded by Queen Eizabeth, so the 1937 winner, Doreen Richer, received it from her in January 1938.

During World War Two the Prize Winners were denied the privilege of going to Sandringham as the Royal Family stayed at Buckingham Palace. The 1942 winner, Betty Bromhead, according to her sister Ann, was so disappointed that many years later she decided to contact Ruth, Lady Fermoy, who as a result, arranged for her and most of the other war-time winners to go to Sandringham to meet the Queen Mother, as she was by then. Unfortunately the 1941 prize winner, Marie Donaldson, had died but fifty years on, in August 1991, Vera Moffatt (Richardson), Betty Webster (Bromhead), Jean Belger (Dunt) and Elizabeth Wharf (Smith), the prize winners from 1940, 1942, 1943 and 1944, finally had their date with royalty. They took with them a copy of *King's Lynn* by Paul Richards and the Queen Mother, while trying to break the sellotape, is reported to have said that she hated 'to spoil the wrapping paper.' One unusual aspect of this story was that Betty was awarded the prize as it normally went to the Head Girl and she was the Deputy. However Ann Bromhead says she was a very popular and outgoing person who had organised many events and so won the votes of the staff and the girls.

As already mentioned, a major innovation in the inter-war period was the production of the School Magazine which was first published in 1923 and was produced every year up to 1939. There was then a gap until July 1944 when a shortened version was produced giving a summary of changes and examination results during the war years to that point. No doubt the fact that Miss Williamson was about to retire encouraged her to put down relevant information and she wrote a short piece on her twenty-five years at the school.

The school crest

The magazine carried information on Speech Days, examination successes, sporting fixtures and results, and reports from the various clubs and societies, as well as from the Girl Guides and Brownies. It printed a large number of articles written by the pupils, including stories, poems and accounts of trips and also carried news of Old Girls and occasional articles about their time at college or about their careers. From Edition Number 2 in 1924 the front cover was to carry the school crest, the figure of St Margaret and the dragon, copied from that on one side of the King's Lynn Corporate Seal, and representing, at least from the school's point of view, the triumph of knowledge and goodness over ignorance and sin. Another useful addition came in Number 10 (1932) when the form lists were printed for the first time, a feature which would continue until 1966.

The main inter-school sports played were hockey and tennis although netball and rounders matches were also arranged. The High School won the Fenland League Tennis Shield in 1921 and then in 1923-4

The 1st XI Hockey team, 1923-24

and won the Fenland Hockey Cup for the first time in the 13 years since the competition began. The other schools involved were Spalding, Wisbech, March and Ely High Schools and Peterborough County School. The school also came second in the Fenland Tennis Tournament that year. Unfortunately in succeeding years this degree of success was not repeated. In 1925-26, for example, the hockey team won only two of its matches and the tennis team came sixth out of the seven schools which took part in the tournament. On a more positive note the school swimming team won the King's Lynn Under-14 Swimming Shield for the second year running and apart from one year held on to it until 1931, after which there is no further mention in the Magazine for some years. The photograph of the successful swimming team from 1924 shows (from left to right) Vera Donaldson, Dorothy Alexander and Norah Johnson with Jessie Billing seated.

In 1931-32, despite the fact that the school team won only five out of its eleven matches during the season and only two out of five in the Fenland competition, the report in the School Magazine said that there had been 'a great improvement in hockey, especially in tactics and combination', but there was 'still room for much improvement and the Fenland Hockey Shield is still to be won by our school'. The reference to a shield as opposed to a cup presumably explains the discrepancy between what was said in 1924 and 1932. Also in 1932 Colours were awarded for the first time. In tennis the school was somewhat more successful. They came third in the main competition and second in the Under-14s in 1932.

Considering the fact that the playing fields were about two miles away and that team members had to give up the Wednesday half day and Saturday mornings for practice and matches it is perhaps not surprising that the school was not renowned for great sporting achievement during this period. However, although the school teams as a whole were not hugely successful, several individuals were chosen to represent Norfolk in hockey, for example, in 1934-35 Ailie Nowell was selected to play for the 1st XI, and two other girls were chosen as reserves. In the following year, 1935-36, four girls were selected to play for the County 1st XI, J Chapman, B Coates, D Carter and J Gay, and one other girl was chosen as a reserve.

That year the school team came top in a Norfolk competition involving four other schools and third in the Fenland League. A year later they went one better coming second in the Fenland League. 1936-37 was also the year when green stockings were introduced to match the green girdles previously worn as identifiers. A 2nd XI hockey team and junior teams were formed to allow more girls to represent the school. That year the school also came joint second in the Fenland Tennis tournament. Things were looking up.

As part of the Hospital Carnival Week in June 1937 there was a highly popular innovation. Twenty girls played in a mixed-doubles tennis tournament with boys from the Grammar School.

During World War 2 the Fenland League matches were discontinued, although some were arranged against Spalding, East Dereham and Ely High Schools and against the Pelicans Ladies'

Swimming Shield winners in 1924

Hockey Team. The annual-mixed doubles tennis tournament also continued and involved boys from the Hackney Downs Grammar School, evacuated to King's Lynn from London, as well as boys from King Edward VII Grammar School.

As is the case in all schools, particular clubs and societies waxed and waned. Some lasted for only a few years and then disappeared, perhaps because of lack of interest, perhaps because a particularly enthusiastic member of staff had left. In the first School Magazine it was reported that there was a Debating Society which had held two meetings, an Art Club which had been in existence for four years and a French Club which after a promising start was dwindling in numbers. A choir had been started in 1921 as had two Guide Companies and a Brownie Pack. According to records at the Girl Guide Headquarters in London one of the guide companies was disbanded as early as 1923 but the other and the Brownie Pack continued until 1932.

In the 1920s and 1930s there was usually an art or sketching club in existence and there are reports from the *Cercle Francais* until 1929. Other clubs which are mentioned in the School Magazine include the Botanical Club from 1925 to 1927 and a History Club in 1937-38. The Debating Society did not last more than a couple of years but interestingly in 1925 the motion 'That co-education is desirable in all secondary schools' was carried by 24 votes to 10, with 3 abstentions. It would take some 54 year to become a reality for the High School girls in King's Lynn.

Some accounts of events in the School Magazine bring an occasion to life. On the morning of 18 October 1924 the school guides and their leader, Miss Watkins, were present at the installation of Prince Henry (later Duke of Gloucester) as the Lord High Steward of Lynn. Unfortunately they were not dismissed until after the Prince had been entertained to lunch by the Mayor and was driven away. The report said that they were 'rather tired but still smiling'. One can really feel sorry for them! I believe the photograph of the guides to have been taken on this occasion.

The Girl Guide Company in about 1924.

There were two clubs which were more long lasting - the Listeners' Club and the Current Affairs Club. The first of these was formed in 1927-28 with the aim of providing the opportunity for girls to enjoy good music. They met every two weeks and listened to vocal and instrumental performances by pupils, staff or visitors. The club was finally wound up in September 1936. At that point it was said that it had been formed before the 'really great days of wireless music and before gramophones had come to perfection'. It had successfully carried out the aims of its founders for some eight years.

The Current Affairs Club was formed in 1930-31 and ran through to the Second World War. Over the years a range of important issues were debated. For example in 1933-34, Germany's withdrawal from the League of Nations and the imposition of a Chinese Emperor in Manchuria by Japan were among the topics which were said to have provoked much discussion. A debate on the motion that 'Germany should be allowed to re-arm' was carried by a small majority. By 1937-38 the issues discussed included Hitler's policy of expansion, the wars in Spain and the Far East and the revolts in Palestine. The following year, in the last School Magazine before the War it was said that the Club was 'now an established part of the Sixth Form curriculum.' It continued during the War, meeting for 40 minutes once a week and a summary of its discussions was pinned up on the notice board.

Although the Current Affairs Club was not up and running in 1926, had it been it would no doubt have discussed the issues surrounding the General Strike. Miss Williamson in her introduction to the School Magazine that summer makes reference to 'a term much disorganised by the absences, late arrivals and early departures caused by a limited train service.'

One new activity which arose directly from shortages of food in World War 2 was the Gardening Club. It was started in 1940 under the guidance of Miss Aylmer, the domestic science teacher. Initially vegetables were grown in Mrs Thomas's garden and on some land at 'The Orchard' in Gaywood, owned by Margaret Boulton's family. Margaret (later Mrs G Bullen) recalls that Miss Aylmer was somewhat stout of figure and was definitely there in a supervisory capacity rather than as a digger! Later Mr J H Catleugh, the Chairman of Governors, had a strip of ground behind the tennis courts at the school playing field ploughed up, although unfortunately the first crop of potatoes was ruined by wire worm. The vegetables grown were sold either to the members of the club or to the school canteen and after the first year some £20 was sent each year to various charities. In 1944, for example, £8 was donated to the Prisoners of War Fund, £2 to the Jubilee Loan Fund, £2 to Dr Barnados, £2 to the Fishermen and Mariners' Royal Benevolent Fund and £2 to Veterinary Aid to Russian Horses. The Gardening Club continued for a few years after the War.

There had been a tradition of raising money for charity for many years, especially for the Children's Country Holiday Fund which was supported every year from at least 1924 when it was reported in the School Magazine that £7 had been collected in the Autumn Term and a further £12 in the Spring Term. And in the last year before World War 2 a large amount was collected for various charities: £16 1s 0d was sent to the Czech Relief Fund; £9 3s 0d to the Baldwin Fund for Refugees; £6 7s 6d to the Eastern Counties Spanish Food Ship; £3 4s 0d to the Earl Haig Poppy Fund; and £14 3s 10d to the Children's Country Holidays Fund.

During the 1920s and 1930s it was only on rare occasions that school plays were put on as stand alone events. Audrey Stratford recounts the production of scenes from *The Taming of the Shrew* in December 1923, when she was on the Lower Sixth. She said it was the first school play for many years, although she could remember a production of *The Tempest* when she first joined the school. The review by Alice Curson in the Magazine refers to Audrey as a 'dashing Lucentio.' The principal role of Kate was played by Joan Ellison, who went on to RADA in 1926. Many years later in the special edition of the Magazine, produced for the 75th anniversary, Joan Cooke (Ellison) recalled rehearsing for the play in the kitchen:

> 'This is imprinted on my memory because of one delightful incident….for the supper scene in which Petruchio flings dishes away when Kate hopes to eat at last we used kitchen plates. Miss Bowman, a very stimulating English mistress, was equally inspiring as a producer. She was demonstrating how Petruchio must work himself into a real show of temper and she flung herself so completely into the part that suddenly kitchen crockery started flying in all directions and but for the restraining hand of another member of staff….I doubt if any of the kitchen service would have survived.'

For the most part, music and drama in the 1920s and 1930s were performed at the annual speech days. In 1933, for example, there were scenes from *A Winter's Tale* and both the school orchestra and a percussion band performed. Up to this date music had largely involved singing or instrumental pieces by individuals or small groups. In 1935 three short plays were acted, two in French and one in Latin. The orchestra also played in 1935 and again in 1936 but was not mentioned in 1937 or 1938 programmes.

Good educational experiences were also provided from early in the 1920s by trips and visits of various kinds. Some were connected with school subjects such as English, art, history or botany; others were to see matches or to take part in guide camps. In 1934 there was a trip to see *Much Ado About Nothing* at the Maddermarket Theatre in Norwich and in 1938 to Stratford-upon-Avon to see *A Midsummer Night's Dream*. Excellent opportunities for the girls to see important works of art were provided by visits to London to see exhibitions of Italian Art in 1930, British Art in 1934 and Chinese Art in 1936. History groups visited Castle Rising and Castle Acre in, for example, 1926, 1932 and 1938. And in the summer of 1925 the newly-formed Botanical Club went to Babingley to collect water plants, to Dersingham because of the variety of heath plants found there and to Leziate to look at fen plants. These local trips would often be made by bicycle at weekends. An England versus Wales hockey match, held in Peterborough, was a popular trip in 1930.

As well as local camps at Heacham the girl guides took part in the Eastern Counties Rally at Culford on 3 July 1926. This was the largest rally that had ever taken place in England with over 6000 guides and brownies present. Both Princess Mary, the President of the Girl Guides Association, and Lady Baden-Powell, the Chief Guide, were at the rally. Only sixteen girls from the High School, together with Miss Ince and Miss Wood, attended the rally because there was a clash with the Fenland Tennis Tournament.

In 1925 sixty girls went to see an exhibition at Wembley and on the way the coach took them to see the City, Trafalgar Square, the Cenotaph, the Houses of Parliament and Westminster Abbey. But perhaps the most unusual trip of this period was the following year when a group went by train to Richmond in North Yorkshire to see a total eclipse of the sun. This involved a somewhat sleepless overnight journey to Darlington as the first leg. At Richmond they used 'eclipsias' to view the sight. Unfortunately clouds prevented them seeing the corona but, according to

Constance Cook in the lower fifth who wrote an account for the School Magazine, the trip was worthwhile just to have experienced the darkness, which she said was 'eerie and quite frightening.' On the return journey they stopped off in York and very much enjoyed a visit to the Minster.

The Old Girls' Association was revived in 1922 and for some peculiar reason at that stage was restricted to those who had left since 1919. It is not clear when this changed, but in 1929 it was reported that several 'older' Old Girls had joined. By the mid-1920s the Association was flourishing. In 1926 there were 85 members and this rose to about 120 the following year. An Old Girls' blazer in navy blue with the school crest in silver and green proved popular and some 50 had been sold by the summer of 1927. The following year a striped navy, silver and green tie was made available. In the 1920s and the early years of the 1930s a range of meetings was organised including sporting events in the summer and a Christmas party. However at a committee meeting in July 1935 it was decided to make some changes to the constitution, for example, members of the upper fifth were to be invited to become junior members of the Association at the reduced subscription of one shilling, compared with 2s 6d for full members. It was also decided that there should be an annual dinner, the first of which was held at the Duke's Head Hotel in October 1935 and was attended by some fifty members of the Association, members of the school staff and the Head Girl and Deputy Head Girl.

The following year, in September 1936, some ninety people, including 68 out of the 127 members of the Association, attended the dinner for what was the first of the Golden Jubilee celebrations. The guest speaker was Mr G H Anderson who had been involved as Clerk to the School Governors (and before that to the Directors of the Graduated County Schools' Association and then the Girls' County School Association) since 1886. He gave an account of the history of the school which was published in the School Magazine the following July. Interestingly he said that he had kept a register of pupils from 1887 which contained to that date some 2800 names. Unfortunately that register does not seem to have survived. Various Old Girls also spoke about their careers, including Audrey Stratford who described her experiences at two international congresses on physiology, one in America and the other in Russia.

In 1937 and 1938 the annual meetings, with refreshments and entertainment, were held in the school and both were well attended. The membership stood at 161 in 1938-39. However because of the War the meeting planned for October 1939 was cancelled and for three years the blackout rules meant that no evening meetings were possible. In any event members were either fully occupied or so scattered that the Association was left in abeyance.

As indicated above, the 50th Anniversary of the founding of the school was celebrated in 1936-37. On 8 July 1937 Speech Day was preceded by a Commemorative Service at St Margaret's Church at which the Bishop of Peterborough was the preacher. A Jubilee Loan Fund, the brain child of Miss Williamson, was inaugurated. The aim was to provide loans to girls to help them train for careers, rather than to go into 'blind alley' occupations at age 16. The idea was that the loans would be repaid when they had obtained suitable posts. Donations were requested from parents, Old Girls and friends of the school. On the following day the school held an Open Day with refreshments, entertainments and competitions, one aim of which was to raise money for the Jubilee Loan Fund. Within a year the fund stood at £224, by 1939 it had increased to £233 and by 1944 to £264. Between 1937 and 1944 loans of £225 had been made, of which £143 had been repaid, leaving £81 still out on loan. As early as 1930 Miss Williamson had spoken about having a loan fund to help older girls to train for various professions and it was said at the time that £50 given to the school by Lord Fermoy in 1929 was to be used for that purpose. However no further mention of this project has been found until 1937.

In September 1939 there was a proposal by the Local Education Authority that the Girls' High School should be closed for the duration of the War and the girls taught in the Grammar School buildings. However Miss Williamson was very much against this idea and persuaded both sets of Governors at a joint meeting to oppose it. Quite soon afterwards boys from Hackney Downs Grammar School were evacuated from London and until the autumn of 1943 they shared the K.E.S. buildings.

What was the situation like during the War Years? Some restrictions have already been mentioned above. However in the special edition of the High School Magazine produced in 1944 it was stated that the war conditions had not greatly interrupted the work of the school. 'It has neither been evacuated nor had to give hospitality to an evacuated school', although a few girls evacuated from London at the beginning of the War were admitted. Alerts were rare and air raids did not occur during school hours. When the alarm siren did sound the girls were instructed to shelter under the desks, not that that would have provided much protection in the case of a hit. According to Mrs Esther Boar (Woodward) who was at the school from 1939 to 1945 there were practice drills when the girls 'retreated from the classrooms to the corridor complete with gas masks.' She says that 'it was a great sin not to have your gas masks with you at all times. If you turned up without it you were sent home again.' Eileen Pleasants (now Mrs Stevenson) who was at the High School from 1940 to 1945 remembers getting off on the wrong foot on her very first day because she had forgotten her gas mask. She was summoned to Miss Williamson's office to be sternly told off and warned that she would be sent home if it happened again.

For a time it was decided to have only morning school but, according to Miss Hilditch this produced 'a ghastly feeling of rush' and 'an atmosphere of terrible frustration'. So after Easter in 1940 normal hours were resumed, albeit with a shortening of the school day in the winter months. The war did result in most school functions, including the annual Speech Day, being abandoned and as indicated above no School Magazine was produced until 1944. According to Eileen Pleasants there were no trips or parties during the war.

Another unfortunate consequence of the War was the decision by the Board of Education and Norfolk Education Committee not to continue with the provision of French assistants in schools, something greatly regretted by the High School Governors 'in view of the benefits derived by senior scholars.' Under Ministry of Defence regulations, place names had to be removed to hinder the enemy in case of an invasion and so in 1940 the name board was removed from the school playing fields. School uniforms were also affected both during wartime and for some years after. In 1941 the President of the King's Lynn Chamber of Trade informed the school that its members were having difficulty complying with school dress regulations in view of clothing rationing.

One positive development was a major expansion in the provision of school meals. These had been first provided in 1924 to about 45 girls. In the summer of 1939 some 70 girls had hot dinners and another 70 brought sandwiches. However in March 1941 the Government decided that it would subsidise school meals so that children would pay only for the cost of the food. As a result, the price went down from 9d to 6d per day and numbers at the High School staying for a school meal went up to 140 in the summer term of 1941, to 190 by September 1942 and a year later to 260. Two shifts were introduced in September 1942 and the following year children in the kindergarten had to be served in the fiction library and some third formers in the domestic science room. By 1944 some twenty girls were also staying for tea because of the cancellation of many trains.

One former student, Daphne Steel (Rudd), in an article in *The Citizen* (02 May 2001), wrote that the school meals were very good. 'Those were the years of food rationing and yet reminisce with any High School girl and we drool over the wonderful school dinners planned and overseen by Miss Aylmer, our domestic science teacher.' In addition Miss Aylmer was responsible for putting on war-time cookery courses for parents. By June of 1940 some 80 people had attended. School meals were not to everyone's taste though. Sheila Nicholson (1933-42) still wrinkles up her nose when she remembers the lentil pie and gravy which was served once per week. Paul Bromhead, who was in the kindergarten from 1939 to 1943, before transferring to K.E.S. where his father, Tom, was a teacher, recalls the 'awful school hot lunches and the smell of cooked cabbage' which put him off cabbage for the rest of his life. In contrast one of his fondest memories is of the 'halfpenny freshly-baked rolls and jam doughnuts available from the baker's shop opposite the school.'

Miss Aylmer was a popular teacher. Cookery was a favourite lesson for Eileen Pleasants who asserts that despite food rationing 'we made lots of lovely dishes' and Miss Aylmer, who she says was 'a very nice but strict teacher….inspired me to love cooking to this day.' There was praise for Miss Aylmer from her colleague, Miss Margery Taylor, Classics Mistress, January 1939 to July 1947. She was greatly impressed by the fact that Miss Aylmer ensured that there was a pancake for every girl on Shrove Tuesday.

During the 1920s and 1930s the staff was relatively static. In most years there were minor changes but many of the staff were there for long periods of time. The longest serving teacher in this period was Miss Ethel Waldegrave who joined the school in 1898 and retired thirty-seven years later in December 1935. Mrs Beatrice Dorer taught classics at the school from 1918 until she retired in December 1938 and again for a short time during the War. Like Ethel Waldegrave she had also been a pupil at the High School, one of the first to be awarded a scholarship at a time when it was essentially a fee-paying school and one of the few university graduates from that period. Her daughters Enid and Emma were both pupils at the High School. When she died in January 1971 she left a water colour by Walter Dexter to the school in her will.

Other long-serving teachers were Miss E M Aylmer (domestic science) 1928-1950, Miss E D Drever (music and eurhythmics) 1928-1942, Miss G M Ince (mathematics) 1921-48, Miss W C Inglis (French) 1922–1941, Miss D Tizzard (art) 1925-42 and Mrs T L Gordon Thomas (mathematics) 1919-44. Some of the other teachers would be at the school long after Miss Williamson retired in 1944: Miss E Beardsell, (history) 1919-1958, Miss G E Green (geography) 1924-56, Miss G M Hilditch (French) 1925-57 and Miss B B Smith (English) 1929-1950.

As we have seen, several long serving staff left either just before the War or during, including Miss Williamson who left in 1944. In a valedictory edition of the School Magazine, an enterprise she had begun in 1923 with edition number 1, she wrote about her twenty-five years as Head Mistress. She recalled that WW1 had somewhat halted the school's development 'very much as the second great war is doing at the moment'. However she acknowledged that her predecessor, Miss Harrison, had left a school which had grown steadily in size and reputation in the thirty years she was in charge.

Miss Williamson and a section of the 1938 school photograph

In the twenty years between the two wars further development had taken place, and she spoke with obvious pride of the addition of the school extension with its archway giving a glimpse of the garden and the river, but also of the cookery room, replacing a number of useless attics at the top of the school house, the biology room, always lively with interesting plants and aquatic creatures, the dining room formed chiefly from the stone-flagged kitchen of the old house, the spacious music room and the library with its well-fitted bookcases.

Miss Williamson recalled how the library and sixth-form work developed side-by-side, how music and eurhythmics took a vital place in the curriculum, how science, practically unknown in 1919, became an integral part of the school course and a subject which girls had been able to continue at university. She pointed out that whereas in the early days a few girls learnt to cook in the science laboratory, now every girl had cookery lessons in a properly-equipped domestic science room. Hundreds of girls had meals at school where formerly some had brought sandwiches. And games, once played by a few, had become, with the purchase of a playing field, a regular part of school life.

She realised that the passing of the 1944 Education Act would have significant effects on the school. In the future all entrants would have to pass an entrance examination and before long fees would no longer be charged.

The 1945 edition of the School Magazine carried a tribute to Miss Williamson by Mrs T L Gordon Thomas who had herself retired at Christmas 1944 after 25 years at the School, the last sixteen of them as Senior Mistress. She referred to Miss Williamson's remarkable powers of organisation and lively sense of humour, 'which must have helped her through many difficult times.' Under her leadership there had been 'quiet, steady work and progress'. That reads like a school report! In 1962, Miss Hilditch, who as well as working under Miss Williamson at the High School for many years had been taught English by her in London, also paid a warm tribute to the former Head:

> 'Miss Williamson was gifted with a clear mind and sound judgement; she would never allow herself to be to be rushed into snap decisions but always insisted on having time for consideration of any matter brought to her notice. She was essentially just in her dealings with staff and girls; she valued highly sound learning and scholarship; above all, she devoted herself with singleness of purpose to the welfare of the school.'

Miss Taylor, also in 1962, said that she had never met any Head Mistress so wise and so able as Miss Williamson. 'She had an uncanny knowledge of every minute happening that occurred in the school. She knew what you were going to think before you thought it and to have told her a lie would have been impossible.' To some of the girls on the other hand, although seen as a fair and just person, she was a remote figure and not very approachable.

Miss Williamson was clearly highly regarded and when she left she was presented with a silver teapot by the Governors, a standard lamp by the teaching staff, a gold wrist watch by the Old Girls' Association, a handbag by the girls at the school and, rather appropriately, a collection of saucepans, dishes and a kettle by the kitchen and cleaning staff.

However a different era was to dawn with the appointment of Miss Winifred Dore who replaced her as Head Mistress in 1944.

4. 1944-68. A breath of fresh air.

Winifred Dore was appointed from a very large field of 170 applicants for the post of Head Mistress. Interestingly the appointing panel included not only Governors and the County Education Officer and his assistant but also Miss Williamson. An outgoing Head would never be involved in the appointment of his or her successor today.

Miss Dore had a 1st Class Honours degree in History from the University of Wales and had been Senior History Mistress at Wimbledon County School for Girls. Much was made in the local press of the fact that at 37 years old she was the youngest Head Mistress in England. According to Daphne Steel (Rudd) in the article already cited, 'When Miss Dore breezed into the Assembly Hall with black gown flying behind her, we felt the winds of change – a breath of fresh air. Yet tradition was respected and any changes were beneficial ones, in keeping with the modern world.'

Miss Winifred Dore in 1944.

She was always smartly dressed and she expected the same of the girls who would be in trouble if shoes were muddy or stocking seams not straight. Although a strict disciplinarian she was seen as fair and kind.

She was also keen to establish high standards of work and high aspirations among the students. She wanted to see increasing numbers going on to higher education and to worthwhile careers. Certainly by the time she retired the sixth form had expanded from about 20 girls in September 1944 to 95 in 1968. In addition overall numbers rose from 364 in 1944 to over nearly 550 in 1962, although they fell back to around 500 by the time Miss Dore retired. The composition of the school population also changed. In 1944 more than half the girls were fee payers but under the 1944 Education Act all fees were abolished. Admissions to the school would in future be on the results of the 11-plus examination set by the County. Also as a consequence of the Act the kindergarten was closed in the summer of 1948 and the other two forms in the preparatory department were phased out, the last pupils leaving in the summer of 1952. The roll fell for a few years after 1948 but started to rise again as numbers in the sixth form increased and, especially from September 1954, when for the first time the school took in the equivalent of three forms into the first year. 87 pupils were admitted compared with 63 in 1953. The photograph from 1955-56 shows how crowded the hall was for morning assembly. By September 1958 when there were three forms in each of the first five years and with a huge intake of 103 pupils the number on roll was 490, including 50 in the sixth form. The situation was to get even more difficult. The 1959 intake of 112 had to be divided into four forms in the first year. The

Morning assembly in 1955-56 (EDP)

hall could no longer take all the girls for assembly and all the first forms had to have prayers in their form rooms.

The rising roll meant that the teaching space was far from satisfactory. At Miss Dore's very first Governors' meeting in October 1944 the need for more accommodation was discussed and in March 1945 the Governors considered plans for school extensions. However they decided that the plans would not provide an adequate solution and they resolved to ask the Local Authority to consider at as early a date as possible the acquisition of a new site and the building of a new High School for Girls. In July of 1947 the Governors were informed that the Local Authority accepted the fact that the school could not be brought up to the standard required by Ministry of Education Building Regulations because the site was too small. It agreed that new buildings should be provided on a new site. However it was anticipated that it would be 1959-60 before this would be possible. Although a new gymnasium was ready on the new site in 1962 it would not be until 1967 that new classrooms and laboratories at Queensway would be opened and when the school was closed in 1979 the King Street site was still in use. Miss Dore stayed on one year longer than she had intended to do in order to oversee the transfer of the Lower School to the new building in 1967-68.

The site which would eventually be used for the new school buildings was acquired in 1951 as a result of an exchange of land. The Local Authority wished to build a new junior school on the

High School playing fields in Estuary Road and agreed to offer land on the Newlyn Estate in exchange and to prepare new playing fields for the school on that site. In 1952 this newly-acquired land was vested in the Official Trustee of Charity Lands. The playing fields started to be used for matches later that year. A major problem was the time wasted travelling between the two sites which meant that the girls had only the equivalent of one period of games compared with two in most other schools, although that was not a new problem.

Throughout her time as Head Mistress Miss Dore had to, in her own words, 'make do and mend' as far as accommodation was concerned. As early as 1946 it was agreed that the Norfolk Fire Service hut on Common Staithe Quay would be used as a canteen. Ten years later there were still two shifts using the hut at lunch time and another two shifts using the Youth Centre in Tower Street. The closure of the kindergarten in 1948 was in one sense opportune. This made possible the doubling in size of the biology laboratory. Previously classes of 25 working for the Higher School Certificate had had to box and cox, half working elsewhere while half did practical work in the laboratory. Further changes took place in 1951 when rooms in the attic on the second floor were converted into a needlework room and a physics room.

In June 1955 plans were approved by the Local Authority for the provision of four additional classrooms and a canteen. However by the middle of the following year it had decided not to go ahead with the original plan. Instead it proposed to erect a science laboratory and a classroom on a site which had been purchased in King Street near the St George's Guildhall (and today used by the King's Lynn Operatic and Dramatic Society.) The new buildings were in use by the autumn term of 1957 but it took until the following summer for the laboratory to be fitted out with proper benches. The Local Authority also began to negotiate for dining facilities in a nearby restaurant. Agreement was reached to use the Vancouver Restaurant, (the former British Restaurant), in New Conduit Street and for ten years from January 1957 the school's kitchen and dining room were located there.

The new kitchen was said to be excellent but Miss Dore complained that the dining room was too cramped and also that there were no cloakroom facilities. For many years she argued that two rooms and cloakroom facilities in the same building used by the Technical College should be made available for use by the school but to no avail.

The former dining room became a needlework room and a room for the lower sixth and in 1958 the old kitchen and scullery were pulled down and this made possible the provision of three additional classrooms. These came into use in the autumn term but in what was initially a quite unsatisfactory state. Even after the provision of these new rooms there were only 11 capable of holding 30 girls and yet there were 15 forms in Years 1 to 5. At this stage some sixth-form lessons were held in two rooms at 3 King Street and small classes such as those for French conversation took place on landings or in the pantry. In 1966 the Local Authority received notice to quit the rooms at 3 King Street and as an alternative five rooms were rented in the YMCA property at 27 King Street known as Shakespeare House. The rooms were smaller than the two previously used but better liked by the upper sixth.

Clearly the only satisfactory long-term solution was the provision of new school buildings. In 1958 the Governors, frustrated by the lack of progress on the provision of adequate accommodation, asked the Local Authority to report on the extent to which the school's site and accommodation fell short of standards laid down by the Ministry of Education. The report when it was delivered in July showed severe deficiencies. The site was some two acres below recommendations for a school of this size, the teaching space was deficient by 7658 square feet, that is about one third below what it should have been, and the area of paved playgrounds was some 27,500 square feet too small. There should have been a gymnasium as well as an assembly hall, nine classrooms were below the statutory minimum of 480 square feet and the domestic science room, the needlework room and the physics laboratory were deemed unsatisfactory. In addition the number of WCs and wash basins was well below requirements.

In February of 1959 the Governors were told that Chief Education Officer accepted the fact that accommodation at the school was unsatisfactory and that he had asked architects to prepare sketch plans for new buildings on the Newlyn site. He agreed that an instalment of the new building was a matter of urgency. Plans for a much needed new gymnasium and changing rooms were prepared later that year and a start was made on the buildings in April 1960. As is often the case with new buildings they were not ready when promised and it was not until on 20 February 1962 that the keys were finally handed over. The following year two temporary classrooms were erected on the site. This allowed about thirty girls to have lessons other than games at Queensway and in 1964-65 it was arranged for them to have lunch at Alderman Catleugh Girls' School to reduce the pressure on the dining room in New Conduit Street which was said to be 'dangerously overcrowded.' In the following year, in order to further relieve the pressure, the upper sixth were allowed to bring sandwiches.

The school had two visits from Ministers of Education during the late 1950s and early 1960s. Mr Geoffrey Lloyd, under pressure to allow the Local Authority to include a new Girls' High School in its building programme paid a surprise visit in March 1958. This must have helped to

Visit by Mr Geoffrey Lloyd in 1958 (LN)

Visit by Sir Edmund Boyle in November 1963 (LN)

Listening to the Minister of Education in 1963 (LN)

The Queensway site in 1967 (LN)

get the first phase of the new building agreed. Certainly a visit by Sir Edmund Boyle on 15 November 1963, when the school 'proudly displayed' its 'cramped conditions', also helped to move things on. Lesley Stevenson (Thain) who was at the school from 1960 to 1967 remembers that all the girls were crowded into the hall although, as we saw above, all the first-year forms were normally excluded from morning prayers.

Soon afterwards it was announced that new buildings were to be included in the 1965-66 building programme, although the school would still be expected to function on the two sites, two miles apart. The Ministry of Education refused to approve the Local Authority plans to complete the new school at an estimated cost of £244,346. Instead it agreed to an instalment, costing some £144,316, which would include an assembly hall, a small hall, eight classrooms, seven practical rooms, a kitchen and ancillary accommodation. The Governors urged the Local Authority to complete the final instalment in the following financial year but were told that this would not be possible. When the new buildings were finally opened in September 1967 the 250 girls in the Lower School were based at the Queensway site leaving a similar number of senior girls at King Street.

Even when Miss Dore gave her last report to Governors in May 1968 not everything was complete. The south-facing rooms at Queensway still did not have blinds, the Head Mistress's room had no curtains and there was no screen or film projector for the hall. She expressed the hope that an additional laboratory and a classroom would be ready for the coming September.

There was an interesting comment in the editorial of the School Magazine in the summer of 1967:

> 'For the lower school an upheaval is pending but probably in their future school career they will have to face a bigger upheaval: that of becoming part of the comprehensive school system.'

In fact it did not affect anyone in the school at the time; it would be another twelve years before it was to become a reality in King's Lynn.

Earlier in April of 1967 a new canteen was opened at King Street to replace that in New Conduit Street. The Norwich Union Insurance Company wanted to acquire the site of the canteen and offered to provide an alternative. After some discussions about the site a pre-fabricated building was put up in Aikmans' Yard next to the Lower Garden and so with direct access to the school. Miss Dore commented that, 'After years of cramped accommodation the school is gaining its new space all at once.' The new canteen was light and airy with good views overlooking the river. It had tables for eight rather than twelve and, very importantly as far as the girls were concerned, it had chairs rather than benches. It came as a great relief after all those years of trailing 'in dismal crocodiles and braving all weathers' to get lunch. Lesley Stevenson (Thain) recalls the fact that the girls assembled in the playground and then made their way to New Conduit Street in the groups of twelve which sat at the same table in the canteen. According to Veronica Woods (1966-70) girls often nipped into a small sweet shop on the way, although this was strictly forbidden.

Miss Dore had a dynamic personality and was highly innovative. During her time as Head Mistress she greatly expanded the opportunities for educational enrichment. Each year there was a programme of visiting speakers, girls were encouraged to go to lunchtime concerts at the Town Hall and in later years at St George's Guildhall, large numbers of trips and visits were organised and drama and musical productions, as well as clubs and societies, were encouraged. Some of the clubs for younger pupils were led by sixth formers who also organised Christmas parties for them. In addition Miss Dore encouraged sport throughout the school and, herself a former Welsh International player, she sometimes played in the staff hockey team.

Unlike Miss Williamson she did not think competition was unhealthy and in 1946 form prizes were introduced. From her first summer at the school there was an Annual Sports Day and in 1947 the competition was enhanced by the introduction of a house system, recommended by HMI as far back as 1923. There were four Houses named after people who had been long associated with the school: Anderson, Brereton, Cresswell and ffolkes: G H Anderson was Clerk to the Directors of the company which originally ran the school and later to the Governing Body until his retirement at the beginning of 1940 after more than 50 years of service; the Reverend JL Brereton could be said to be the founder of the school in 1886/87, although as we saw in Chapter 1 his association with it lasted only a little over a year; Mrs Eva Cresswell was one of the original Directors of the County School for Girls when it was founded in 1887 and remained a Governor until her death in 1942; the fourth house was named after the Rev. Sir Francis ffolkes, a

Presentation of the Vixtrix Ludorum Rose Bowl to Joy Suckling by Alderman J H Catleugh in 1956

Governor for 29 years until just a few months before his death in 1938, and Chairman since 1921.

For several years the main competition was that which took place on Sports Day and the most successful competitor on the day became the Victrix Ludorum. The photograph shows Joy Suckling (1950-56), now Mrs Joy Barber, receiving the silver rose bowl from Chairman of Governors, Mr J H Catleugh. She was allowed to keep the trophy for the following year and also received a small silver cup which she still has in her possession. Over the years additional house competitions were added, such as those for hobbies, speech, general knowledge and cross country.

The new school berets in 1948

Because of increasing numbers in the school, from the beginning of the Spring Term in 1960, the house system was changed and the girls were allocated to eight new houses, each for about 65 pupils, and named after famous women - Jane Austin, Elizabeth Blackwell, Marie Curie, Elizabeth Fry, Amy Johnson, Florence Nightingale, Emmeline Pankhurst and Mary Slessor.

Unfortunately for four years, from 1962 to 1965, the school did not hold its own sports day and so for a time that element of competition was lost.

Another innovation was the introduction of a School Council in 1949-50. The idea was that members of the School Council would learn how meetings should be conducted and also gain some experience of how democracy worked. Each form elected two representatives who met with Miss Dore to discuss issues raised by pupils. As one might imagine, school uniform was regularly discussed, although a major change had already taken place in 1948 when the beret was introduced as an alternative to the velour hats. This proved very popular at the time although it became a favourite hate in later years. Other changes were made at later dates, for example in 1963 girls were allowed to put a two inch strip of cardboard inside the berets to give them a 'pillbox ' look made fashionable by Jackie Kennedy. The uniform had to be bought from Catleughs, the outfitters, and each new girl went with her parents armed with a long list of necessary items. This was still the case in the 1970s when Julie Dixon (Bunting) was at school. She describes the assistant going 'from one glass-fronted drawer to another via a wooden step-ladder assembling a massive pile on the counter, from the bright green science overall…. to the unfeasibly large bottle-green knickers.' It must have been a large outlay for many families. All

Miss Dore and the Prefects 1947-48

Miss Dore and the Prefects 1957-58

items of uniform had to be clearly labelled.

As mentioned above sixth formers were encouraged to take responsibility for running clubs for younger pupils. The prefects were also seen as important in the maintenance of school discipline and setting standards of good conduct. They were led by a Head Girl and a Deputy Head Girl up to 1953-54. However from the following year a different Head Girl was chosen each term. No explanation of this has been found, although Miss Dore presumably decided that the new arrangement gave more girls the chance to show leadership qualities.

A geography trip to the Lake District in 1961

Opportunities to go on trips and visits were a regular feature of the school before the War. However during Miss Dore's time the number and range was even greater than before. They included annual trips such as those to Castle Acre and Castle Rising for second or third year pupils led by Miss Beardsell. There were geography trips including local ones to the Lynn docks

A visit to the Olympic Games in 1948

or Hunstanton or residential field courses such as those to the Lake District, Swanage and Snowdonia led by Miss Carey and later by Miss Breeze. There were biology field trips such as those to Blakeney and biology students, like the geographers, also attended residential field courses provided by the Field Studies Council. The opportunity to see live performances was considered very important and so there were regular theatre trips to Cambridge, Norwich, London and Stratford. And as well as plays there were sometimes opportunities to go to the ballet or to concerts, for example in May 1949 the Sadler's Wells Ballet and the LSO under Sir Malcolm Sargent both performed in Peterborough and so trips were arranged. Regular visits to London art galleries and museums were also organised. Those keen on sport were also catered for by trips to see international hockey matches. One particularly special trip was that to the London Olympics in June 1948. Pamela Woodward (1942-49), now Mrs Cross, remembers watching the javelin competition and the hurdles races. She says that they had to wear a school blazer and a dress with green in it. Because of the need for clothes coupons the

A trip to the Festival of Britain and Houses of Parliament in 1951

rule about the green and white striped dresses which were part of the summer uniform was not strictly enforced at that time.

A rather unusual trip was enjoyed by over 50 fifth and sixth formers who in March 1949 went to see the wedding presents given to Princess Elizabeth, as she was then, and Prince Phillip in 1948. The girls were later divided into two groups, one going to the National Gallery and the other to the Houses of Parliament. The latter were given a conducted tour by Major Frederick Wise, the MP for Lynn, who also arranged for them to sit in the public galley of the House of Commons, where they heard Harold Wilson, then the President of the Board of Trade answering questions. Little did they know that he would one day be Prime Minister. They saw some well-known people including the then Prime Minister, Mr Clement Atlee, and also Mr Winston Churchill. After listening to question time the girls were entertained to tea by Major Wise. Those who went to the National Gallery perhaps felt they were hard done by. A number of trips to London took place in future years and the photographs show groups outside the Houses of Parliament, with Major Wise in 1951 and Mr Derek Page MP in 1965.

Every year from July 1954 the fourth forms were taken on what was a highly educational trip to Derbyshire and Stratford. All the girls in the year went on the trip. Money was raised at school fetes and from other sources to pay for those who could not afford it. The party was divided into two halves, one half going first to Derbyshire and the other group starting in Shakespeare country, where Miss Dore was based. A number of other staff accompanied the girls when travelling. The itinerary varied somewhat from year to year but in Stratford usually involved seeing two

A trip to the Houses of Parliament in 1965

plays and visiting places associated with Shakespeare and the girls had the opportunity to see actors whose names are still well known today. The cast of *A Midsummer Night's Dream* in 1959, for example, included Albert Finney, Robert Hardy, Vanessa Redgrave, Charles Laughton and Ian Holm.

In Derbyshire the limestone scenery of the Winnats Pass, the stalactites of Treak Cliff Cavern, the Stepping Stones in Dovedale and stately homes such as Chatsworth and Haddon Hall were among the attractions included. I particularly like the story told by Val Hawkins (Jaggs) about Miss Carey's response when a girl asked her what they would do if it rained. She was told that they would do all the things they had planned to do but with a raincoat on!

On the journey between Stratford and Derbyshire the Cadbury Factory and model village at Bournville were visited. Over the years the School Magazine carried many descriptions of these trips. However in 1966 the article consisted simply of quotations of which the following are just a selection: the highlight was Chatsworth House; I particularly enjoyed walking along Dovedale and Monsal Dale; the Treak Cliff Caverns were fascinating; Derbyshire was breathtaking; David Warner as Hamlet was perfect; Michael Jayston *talked* to us; I had no idea Shakespeare could be so exciting; an unforgettable experience; I shall remember it all my life. What splendid tributes. When Miss Dore and Miss Green organised the first such trip they could not have known it would become a regular feature of the extra-curricular programme for so many years to come. Many

The group which spent a holiday in Switzerland in 1955

people have told me what an excellent experience that trip provided.

Foreign trips also became a popular feature of the extra-curricular provision. The first trip abroad was to Switzerland led by Miss Dore during August 1949, Several more were to follow, although a proposed trip in the summer of 1953 had to be cancelled because of a French rail strike. The photograph shows the party taken to Switzerland in 1955. Other trips included ones to Paris in the early 1950s led by Miss Hilditch and in later years by Miss Lewton Brain and Miss P Smith. There were also trips to Florence and Rome in 1962 and to Austria in 1963 and 1968. The latter was one of the first ski trips organised for the girls of the High School. For a number of years girls took part in educational cruises, the first of which was in March 1965, when a party of 80 girls and five staff visited a number of historic sites in the Mediterranean on *The Devonia*, a converted troop ship. The pupils were flown to Genoa where they boarded the ship. The first stop was Naples from where they visited Pompeii; from Naples the ship sailed via Stromboli, an active volcano, and through the Straits of Messina to Greece and for many girls the visits to Athens and to Delphi were the highlights of the trip. From Pireaus, the port of Athens, the ship took the girls to Corfu and finally up the Adriatic coast to Venice from where they flew home. Also from the early 1960s foreign exchange trips to France and Spain were organised.

Susan Ely (1958-65), now Mrs Williams, took part in the trip to Stratford and Derbyshire in 1962, the holiday to Austria in 1963 and the educational cruise in the Mediterranean on *The Devonia* in 1965. Sue won the Old Girls' Association Senior Essay Prize for her account of the visit to Athens and she acknowledges the value of such experiences below:

'Now I look back I realise with hindsight how much I owe to these trips and how they broadened my outlook....I owe a great deal to the education I received at the High School and to the foresight of those who encouraged extra-curricular activities.'

She has some fascinating memories of the trips. I particularly like her story of the visit to the Hellbrunn Palace in Saltzburg famous for its trick fountains:

'Water was the central theme in the palace's design. Hidden in the shade of bushes and trees, or jetting out from unexpected places, the world famous Wasserspiele have been the main attraction at Hellbrunn for 400 years. The most vivid image I have is of the stone 'picnic' table and slab seats where guests were expected to entertain the Prince Archbishop, but when he grew bored by their rhetoric he could switch on the water jet beneath their seats and soak them to the amusement of all present. As we toured the gardens and grottos we were all subjected to such treatments as we unknowingly trod on the water triggers. It was great fun for a group of teenagers.'

Sue also makes the point when writing about the trip to Austria in 1963 that attitudes towards risk were much more relaxed in those days:

'Another amazing memory I have of this trip which highlights how attitudes have changed, is that one day we set off on a hike from the hotel into the mountains and after half an hour I began to feel faint and uncomfortable. Clearly I could not continue but the alternative was for the whole group to return. One of the teachers walked to the road side and flagged down the first car that appeared – a German couple. She asked them to drop me off at the hotel which was on their route down the mountain. I duly got into the car and ten minutes later was back on familiar ground; I could not speak German but managed to nod and smile thanks.'

No harm had been done, but it could not happen today.

Some of the clubs and societies which had existed before and during the War, such as the Current Events Club and the Gardening Club, continued for a time. New ones were started but some did not last long. In 1944-45 a sixth-form art group was responsible for some murals which were completed on the walls of the art room, although a more spectacular one, measuring 22 feet by 6.5 feet was completed in 1948-49 by Jill English and Margaret Lumsden. Soon after the War a Literary and Debating Society was formed, although the meetings were largely devoted to play readings. However it did hold three debates as well as play readings in 1945-46. A French Club started in 1946 was still running in 1955, albeit with some gaps. The Science Club formed in the summer of 1947 held six meetings during the following school year but does not seem to have survived the poorly-attended session in which 'members tried their hand at dissecting frogs'. A Swimming Club was formed in May 1947 and that year had 80 members.

In 1954-55 several new clubs were formed: a Sketch Club, a Hobbies Club, a Local Knowledge Club and a resurrected Debating Society. The Local Knowledge Club continued for many years and was run by sixth formers for younger pupils. In 1959-60, for example, there were visits to the Lynn News, Campbell's Soups, the Post Office, the Police Station and the Royal Stud. A branch of the Christian Union was formed in 1953-54 and ran for several years before being replaced by meetings of the Student Christian Movement.

As we saw in the last chapter the school Guide Company was disbanded in 1932. In the 1950s some High School girls belonged to the St Margaret's Guides' Company which was run by Miss

A guide camp at Sheringham in 1954

Taylor (not a member of staff) and Miss Carey. The photograph shows nine third year girls at the 1954 Guide Camp at Sheringham: Janet Curtis, Shirley Meers, Linda Barnwell (not KLGHS), Liz Gamble, and Evelyn Hefferman on the back row from left to right; and Fay Cullum, Ann Ely, Janet Roper and Margaret Allen on the front row.

One important innovation was the formation in February 1948 of the 1st King's Lynn (High School) Cadet Company with ten members under the leadership of Miss Leach and Miss Sauvain. The very worthwhile aim was to enable ex-Girl Guides to train to be Guiders. Such groups are very dependent on staff willing to take the lead and records show that the company was disbanded in December 1955.

A major change during this period was the introduction of several clubs and societies which encouraged the mixing of High School girls and boys from the Grammar School. In 1956-57 an Inter-Sixth form Society, also known as the 30-30 Club, was formed and this continued right

Barrie's Quality Street in 1950

through to 1968 and beyond, although it was better attended in some years than others. There were social events, talks, debates and film shows. In 1957-58 High School girls attended meetings of the Grammar School Jazz Club. From 1958-59 there was also a Ballroom Dancing Club which was held at the Grammar School until 1963-64 when it was transferred to the High School. That seemed to have resulted in enthusiastic participation by fourth form girls but fewer senior ones. A Reels Club at which Scottish Dances were taught by Mr Hales at the Grammar School on Saturday evenings was popular for a couple of years in the early 1960s. Another joint venture was the Geographical Society was formed in 1965-66.

Other clubs which came and went during the 1950s and 60s included a History and Geography Society, Senior and Junior Music Clubs, an Art Club, a Gymnastics Club, a Film Club, a Junior Society offering a range of activities to younger pupils, Drama Clubs for different year groups and Senior and Junior Modern Educational Dance groups.

In 1967-68, because of the problems caused by the split site, clubs were difficult to organise but there was a Film Club at the Queensway site and a newly-formed Christian Fellowship Society which held a variety of meetings, including joint ones with the Grammar School and the Technical College. The topics ranged from a talk entitled 'Hell, Fire and Brimstone' to a film about the persecution of Christians in East Germany. The Inter-Sixth Form Society continued to meet and as well as social events there were talks on wines, the theatre and the 'Red Guard in Modern Britain.'

Drama in the 1950s and 1960s flourished. The first full-length play put on for many years was J M Barrie's *Quality Street* performed in June 1950. In the autumn term a Literary and Dramatic Society was formed and members of the group put on a well-received performance of the tea party scene from Shaw's *Pygmalion* later in the year. Their first major production was of *Twelfth*

King's Lynn Charter Pageant 1954

Night performed in the Guildhall on two nights in November 1951. Music was provided by the School Orchestra under Mr S T Phillips.

In the Spring Term of 1954 members of the Dramatic Society were involved in the King's Lynn Charter Pageant which was performed on five days from Tuesday to Saturday following a dress rehearsal on the Monday. The High School girls took part in an enactment of the opening of the Mart in the eighteenth century which also involved the Mayor, Deputy Mayor, Aldermen and several Councillors. Katherine Sauvain took the part of Fanney Burney.

Later that year there was the first of a very successful series of joint productions with boys from King Edward VII Grammar School of Gilbert and Sullivan operas. *Iolanthe*, produced by Mr Whitmarsh-Knight and Miss Dore was performed in the Guildhall on four nights at the beginning of December 1954. 'At last we were free from the serious disadvantage of girls acting the parts of men' was the heartfelt cry in the School Magazine. Jean Simpson as Iolanthe, Marion Hardy as the Fairy Queen, Angela Rose as Phyllis, Tim Riley as Strephon and Lew Higdon as the Lord Chancellor all gave good performances, according to the review, but the chorus singing was 'occasionally weak.' Other joint productions followed: *HMS Pinafore* in 1957 and 1965; *The Gondoliers* in 1959 and 1967; *Pirates of Penzance* in 1961; and *Iolanthe* once again in 1963. It is remarkable that school productions could be staged so successfully in the Guildhall over many years.

Flushed with success and enthusiasm from the production of *Iolanthe*, in December 1954, a performance of *Tobias and the Angel* by James Bridie was staged on two days in March 1955. This was followed by Bernard Shaw's *Androcles and the Lion* in 1956, *Much Ado about Nothing* in March 1958, *Sheridan's School for Scandal* in 1960, *A Midsummer Night's Dream* in 1962, *The Lady's not for Burning* by Christopher Fry in 1964, Sheridan's *The Rivals* in 1966 and

Iolanthe 1954

Antigone by Sophocles in 1968.   Apart from the last two, these plays were produced by Miss Passmore, who was also responsible for encouraging form drama as well as poetry reading and speech competitions.   The girls' dramatic talent was recognised more widely in June 1967 when

Pirates of Penzance 1961 (LN)

HMS Pinafore, 1965

The Gondoliers, 1967 (EDP)

three girls, Nancy Vernon as Viola, Christine Reed as Maria and Lorraine Spriggs as a Lady in Waiting, took part in a Norfolk Schools' production of *Twelfth Night* at Norwich Castle. In March 1967 the Senior and Junior Drama Groups combined to perform a dance-drama, *The Martyrdom of Thomas Becket.*

The Gilbert and Sullivan operas involved large numbers of participants but other forms of music seem to have involved only small numbers of pupils. For many years both individuals and groups took part in the annual King's Lynn Music Festival. In 1945 this was held at Gaywood Park School and the guest conductor was Stanford Robinson, a radio presenter and conductor of the BBC Theatre Orchestra. A concert which was open to the public was held in the afternoon. Another musical highlight was the participation of a small group of girls from the High School in the Second National Festival of Schools' Music in May 1951. The massed choirs performed at the Albert Hall with the Royal Philharmonic Orchestra under Sir Adrian Boult.

Although in 1944 a small orchestra of violinists was formed under Miss Carter, in the early post-war years there are few other mentions in the School Magazine. Its numbers waxed and waned in the 1950s and 1960s. We have seen above that an orchestra under Mr Phillips provided the music for the production of *Twelfth Night* in 1951, but two years later there were only nine members including violinists and recorder players. In 1958-59 there was an orchestra some 20 strong under Miss Willden but for the performances of *Pirates of Penzance* in 1961 music was provided by Anne Pratt (1955-61), now Mrs Greeves, and Miss Duggan on the piano. However two years later a combined orchestra from the High School and K.E.S. and bolstered by only three adults played the music for the production of *Iolanthe*. It was said to be a 'big triumph.' The combined orchestras also played an extract from Bizet's Arlesienne Suite in the annual King's Lynn Music Festival in June 1963 and were placed 2nd. In the same competition the High School Choir gained 1st place in the madrigal section.

Androcles and the Lion 1956 (EDP)

School for Scandal 1960 (LN)

The School Choir under Miss Duggan in 1965

The following year, having lost their conductor, Mr Bassett, numbers in the orchestra fell. However they still managed to play an overture to *The Lady's not for Burning* and a 15 minute slot at Speech Day. The School Choir that year, under Miss Duggan, took part in a range of events, including the King's Lynn Choral Society's performance of Haydn's *Creation.* After a gap the orchestra was re-established in 1965-66 under Mr Peace, the peripatetic strings teacher, and the following year played at the Carol Service, on Speech Day, at Dersingham Secondary Modern School and in the King's Lynn Music Festival. In 1967-68 it suffered from the division of the School, leaving only six members at King Street. However the juniors at Queensway were enthusiastic and the combined orchestras performed as usual at the Carol Service and on Speech Day.

As we saw above, until the early 1950s, the playing fields were to the left of what is now Edward Benefer Way where St Edmund's School is situated today. For games lessons the girls together with the equipment were taken by bus to and from the fields. However on Saturday mornings when there was an inter-school match the teams had to make their own way to the grounds. June Howling (Smith) recalls how she and her friend Ann Burton (Horner) shared a bicycle. June came into Lynn from Terrington and walked to her friend's shop at the end of New Conduit Street from where Ann would set off on her bicycle and June would set off to walk. At about half way to Estuary Road the bicycle was left for June to ride the rest of the way. They made the return journey in the same way.

Hockey and tennis continued to be the main sports played at the school. In hockey, as before the War, the teams competed in the Fenland League and in two one-day tournaments, one for Fenland schools and the other for Norfolk grammar schools. Success was mixed. However in 1947-48 the 1st XI won the Fenland Tournament held at Peterborough and came second in the League, while in the Norfolk tournament both the 1st XI and 2nd XI were placed second. The following year was said to be 'undoubtedly the best on record' since all members of the 1st XI were selected to represent Norfolk in either the County 1st (Pat Williams, Pat Goodale, Ann Horner, Marian Lake, Janice Petts and Stella Jones) or 2nd teams (Joy Hodge, Joan Kirkland, Jill Trenowath, Pat Watson and Sheila Gore). The school 1st XI were joint first in the Fenland League and second in the Fenland Tournament.*

Often the 1st XI did better in the Norfolk competition than against the stronger Fenland teams, for example in the four years 1950-51 to 1953-54 although they were placed first or equal first in the Norfolk Tournament in Norwich they only came third or fourth in the Fenland League. 1962-63 and 1963-64 were both successful years. In the first the school won both the Norfolk competition and the Fenland League Tournament and the following year managed to retain the second of the trophies. Although the 1st XI did not retain the Norfolk Schools' Cup the U15 XI did win their section of the competition.

The real grudge match of the year was that against the Grammar School. Anne Pratt, who was the 1st XI team goalie for several years, remembers it always being a very hard fought match, so much so that on one occasion a boy's stick was broken in half. She also recalls that the boys often lifted the ball, something that later became a penalty offence.

* During the year Betty Bunting replaced Joy Hodge as the goalie.

The triumphant 1948-49 hockey team

As already mentioned, individual players were regularly selected to play for County teams. In 1949-50 eight members of the school 1st XI played in the Norfolk 1st XI and one of them, Sheila Gore, was selected to play in the successful East Anglian team which toured Holland in the Easter holidays and won all the matches. In 1953-54 Stella Rose captained the Norfolk 1st XI as did Ruth Johnson ten years later. Stella went on to be hockey captain at Sheffield Training College in 1956-57. In 1964-65 seven girls were selected to play for County teams, four of them, Janet Grief, Ruth Charlesworth, Angela Loades and Diane Nurse for the 1st XI and three others for the 2nd XI.

Girls were particularly proud to be awarded School Colours. These were indicated by braid around the edge of the school blazer. In the 1950s and early 1960s the Colours were green for hockey and white/cream for tennis. If a girl was awarded both then the colours would be intertwined. Shelagh Wallace (1947-53), now Mrs Perham, who was awarded both, in later years played hockey for Middlesex.

The 1954-55 tennis team

The 1956-57 tennis team

The school tennis teams tended to be less successful than the hockey teams, only once achieving better than fourth place out of seven in the Fenland Tennis Tournament in the late 1940s and early 1950s. However in 1955 the school tennis team, captained by Joan Whittell, won the Tennis Shield for the first time since 1921. Two years later the Seniors again won the Fenland Tennis Tournament and the Juniors were placed second. However in subsequent years school teams had rather less success. There is no doubt that the frequent changes in games staff had a detrimental effect on the school's performance in sporting competitions, especially in the late 1950s and early 1960s.

Other sports such as athletics became more popular from the late 1950s and there were some outstanding individual successes. For three years running, from 1957, Ann Simpson was Victrix Ludorum at the school Sports Day. In the same three years she was selected to represent Norfolk in the hurdles at the All-England Athletics Championships. Joy Donald (in 1957) and Pearl Smith (in 1959) were also selected to take part in the Championships. For some reason no Sports Days were held in the years 1962-65. However normal service was resumed in 1966. After the Town Sports Day that year five girls were selected to compete in the County Sports at Norwich. Diane Nurse came 2nd in the Senior Discus competition and three others were placed 3rd in their events. The following year the school entered a full team for the Town Sports for the first time and 11 girls were selected to represent King's Lynn in the Norfolk Athletics Championships. Earlier in the Spring term the school entered a team in the King's Lynn and District Cross Country Championships and four of the senior girls went on to run in the National Schoolgirls' Cross Country Championships in Rochdale.

Every year from 1962 to 1968 the school won the Woodwark Shield for the best team at the King's Lynn Swimming Gala. In the summer of 1963 High School girls broke three records and won every event except one. In 1967 13 girls went on to represent King's Lynn in the Norfolk Swimming Gala and two represented the County in the Eastern Area Championships in Chelmsford. The following year 11 girls represented King's Lynn in the Norfolk Swimming Gala and all gained a 1st, 2nd or 3rd place in at least one event. Some of the best swimmers in the late 1960s included Mary Ann Robinson, Linda and Anne Gillies and Judith Alcock.

Towards the end of Miss Dore's time as Head Mistress the range of sporting activities grew considerably. In 1966-67, in addition to hockey, tennis, swimming and athletics, the School Magazine also carries reports on dance, netball, rounders, volleyball and badminton. Sport was becoming even more high profile.

Throughout this period, as before the War, the girls were encouraged to raise money or give provisions to those less fortunate than themselves and to support other good causes. Each year, for example, the produce brought to the Harvest Festival was taken to an Old Folk's Club. Sixth formers would sort out all the produce and make up bags including a selection of each item where possible. The sixth formers would also provide some musical entertainment to the club members, usually accompanied on the piano by Mrs Dorothy MacDonald.

As mentioned above, the play put on in June 1950 was J M Barrie's *Quality Street*. The proceeds, together with those from a bring-and-buy sale and fair and from a gymnastics display, allowed

Sixth formers at the Old Folks' Club in 1949

Visit by the Queen Mother and Princess Margaret in 1951 (LN)

the school to sponsor two seats in the restored St George's Guildhall at a cost of 100 guineas each. The names of donors were originally placed on the back of the seats and although these were later removed the list of donors can still be seen on a board at the back of the auditorium. The bulk of the money, some £150, was raised by the bring-and-buy sale and fair organised by Head Girl, June Smith. Each form was asked to provide a fund-raising stall and this effort proved very successful. Another school fair in March 1960 raised £100 of which £50 was sent to the World Refugee Fund and £50 to the King's Lynn Preservation Trust. One further example of charity fund raising is the £55 16s raised to buy coal for old people at Christmas 1965.

Visits to the High School by Ministers of Education have already been mentioned and Miss Dore was able to secure some very distinguished guests to present prizes at Speech Day each year. One planned visit which did not take place was in May 1948 when Princess Margaret was unable to attend because of an attack of measles. However she did accompany the Queen on an unofficial visit to the school on 7 February 1951. They had been to see the restoration work done on the St George's Guildhall and Mr Catleugh, who was accompanying the royal party, suggested that they might like to see the river from the summer house in the garden of the High School. Such an unexpected visit clearly caused a great deal of excitement among the girls. According to the editorial in the Magazine, 'Anyone who claimed that Her Majesty had spoken to her was treated with reverent awe for some time afterwards.' The following extract from an account by P Lowery in 3s demonstrates the unexpected nature of the visit:

'We were quietly working in the Science Laboratory when suddenly in rushed a breathless Joy Hodge. She gave her message to Mrs Baker and dashed out of the room. Mrs Baker then …. told us to line up in twos beside the door. Feeling very mystified we obeyed. I asked Gillian if she knew what was happening. You can imagine my surprise when she answered, 'The Queen!'….

As we passed through the Hall we saw a jumble of gym clothes on the floor, showing plainly the haste with which their owners had discarded them. At last we were in the playground and there we saw long rows of school girls all looking in one direction. When we were neatly in our rows we also looked in that direction….and there we saw the Queen herself talking to Mr Catleugh and looking at the girls.'

One can only wonder what Miss Dore's first thoughts were when told that the Queen would be at the school shortly!

Queen Elizabeth had a long association with the school and presented more Queen's Prizes than either of her predecessors – 45 in the period from 1937 to 1979 alone. As mentioned in the previous chapter there were no personal presentations during the War but in January 1946 Minnie Drewery, the 1945 winner, was accompanied by Miss Dore to Sandringham where she was received by Queen Elizabeth. In this period the prize was awarded for Service to the School and as in previous years the winner was chosen on the vote of the girls and the staff.

June Smith (1943-50) was awarded the prize in 1950 and like other winners she has treasured her leather-bound volume of *The English Parnassus: an anthology of longer poems*. The photographs show her with her prize in 1950 and as Mrs June Howling in 2011. Occasionally two girls were awarded the prize as in 1957 and 1964 when the winners were Diana Ducker and Janet Turner and Vivienne Browne and Joy Waterworth respectively. However in 1965 although

June Smith and friends at Sandringham January 1951

June Howling (Smith) 2011 (M Walker)

the Queen Mother's Treasurer agreed to increase the value of the prize to £10 5s the school was asked not to award more than one prize in any year.

A change in the name of the prize took place after the death of King George VI and the accession of Queen Elizabeth ll to the throne. A letter to Miss Dore from Canon W R Musselwhite, the Rector of Sandringham, in July 1952 said that 'Her Majesty felt strongly that this presentation was very personal to Queen Elizabeth the Queen Mother' who would be happy to continue it. However in future it would be known as Queen Elizabeth's Prize. The first winner of the newly-named prize was Hilary Dodd in 1952 and the Queen Mother continued to present it, albeit to a student at Springwood High School from 1980, until her death in 2002, when it once again became The Queen's Prize.

In fact up to 2002 the prize had always been the Consort's prize for a High School girl, a parallel prize to the Gold Medal awarded each year since 1864 to a boy at the Grammar school. When Princess Alexandra became Queen in 1901 the prize was named after her and it was known as Queen Mary's Prize from 1926 to 1936.

Miss Dore was keen to make people aware of the history of the school and in the early 1950s introduced the tradition of having a Founders' Day Service and entertainment on 26 January, the date mentioned by the Reverend J L Brereton as being the first day of term of the new school for girls in 1886. She also ensured that important anniversaries did not go unnoticed. We saw in the previous chapter the 50th anniversary of the founding of the school was celebrated in 1936-37. Miss Dore decided that the 75th anniversary should be similarly marked. Three special events were planned over two days in 1962. On Friday 20 July there was a Thanksgiving Service at St Nicholas Chapel at which the Bishop of Grantham gave the address. Later that day the school was open to allow former students to look around and see any changes that had been made since they were there. Refreshments were provided in the hall and Miss Dore gave an illustrated talk on the history of the school. Afterwards the film produced by Mrs Gordon Thomas in 1937 was shown, followed by some colour slides and a short film of the school in 1962. On the following day an Anniversary Dinner was held in the Town Hall for former staff and students, some whom had attended the school early in the twentieth century. Very importantly a special edition of the School Magazine was produced which included a brief section on the early days of the school (1886-1914), reminiscences written by former pupils and staff, many of them very detailed, and up-to-date information on about 100 old girls.

How successful was the High School academically during the period of Miss Dore's headship? From 1945 to 1950 the main examinations were still the School Certificate (SC) and the Higher School Certificate (HSC). During these six years the number of successful candidates at the lower level was between 32 and 42 and at the higher level between five and eight. Only one or two students a year achieved the grades to be awarded scholarships to pay for a university education, although a greater number went on to teacher training colleges. In 1947 two went on to university and six to colleges, in 1948 it was one and ten and in 1949 four and nine. Some of the girls going on to training colleges went direct from the lower sixth as the entry requirements did not include passes in the HSC.

The General Certificate of Education introduced in 1951 differed from its predecessor in that it was a single-subject examination. In the early years of the examination the students at both levels were graded from 1 to 9 with grades 1 to 5 being passes and grades 6 to 9 failures. However in 1960 a change was made so that grade 6 at both levels became a pass. In the analysis of results the school reported the percentage of grades 1-3 as 'Good Passes'. From 1963 a further change occurred at A' Level when the pass grades were re-labelled A-E.

Inevitably results were better in some years than others. At Advanced Level the percentage pass rate was as high as 87% in 1958 with an outstanding 42% in the top three grades, whereas the comparable figures for 1954 were 67% and 22%. In the latter year all five candidates entered for mathematics failed. Results after 1961 were generally better than in the 1950s with a pass rate of over 80%. However this may have been because candidates who were unlikely to pass were not entered. In 1963, for example, when the pass rate was an excellent 84%, with 35% graded A or B, there were 10 students who passed in three subjects, 8 in two subjects and 4 in one subject. Miss Dore when reporting the results to the Governors did not hold back any critical comments. In 1961, when the pass rate was 70%, she referred to the results in chemistry and physics as 'lamentable'.

At the beginning of Miss Dore's final year at the High School some ten girls were hoping to gain university places, two were aiming for places at Colleges of Advanced Technology and sixteen wanted to enter teacher training. Numbers were certainly higher than in the past but were still at a relatively modest level.

There were of course some outstanding individual successes. The earliest to be reported was former student Joan Bentley who left school in 1942 to work at the John Innes Laboratory in Norwich. In 1945 she was awarded the Royal Horticultural Society's Gold Medal, having been placed first in its national examination, open to both men and women. In 1953 Cynthia Wright was awarded a Ministry of Agriculture Senior Scholarship. In 1955 Ann Coulton gained a place at Girton College, Cambridge and in 1958 Jennifer Searle was awarded an Exhibition in History at the same college. Also in 1958 Lesley Perry took up a place at Newnham College, Cambridge and Edelgard Rickert was awarded an Exhibition by Westfield College, London. In 1959 Elizabeth Gamble took up a place to read PPE at Somerville College, and became the High School's first girl at Oxford. In 1960 Moira Coleman was awarded a Reid Scholarship at Bedford College, London and in 1962 Judith Richardson the Pfeiffer Scholarship to the same college.

1963 was a typical year in terms of university entries with five students gaining places, including Helen Hamson who won a Mathematics Scholarship to Queen Elizabeth College in London, now part of King's College, and Diane Parr who gained a place to read English at St Anne's College, Oxford.

Some of the young women followed up success in their first degrees with research. In 1956, for example, Lorna Lilly, with a Ph.D from Sheffield University under her belt, gained a post in the Genetics Department at the University of Glasgow. Another to follow an academic career was Heather Beaumont. Having gained a degree in Zoology at Nottingham University, she was awarded a Medical Council research grant to work under Sir Solomon Zuckerman in the School of Medicine at Birmingham University and was awarded a Ph.D in 1961.

There were also successes in various competitions. In 1956 Ruth Coulton won a Field Services Scholarship which allowed her to spend a year in California before taking up a place at the University of Manchester. Ruth was also the 1956 winner of the Queen Elizabeth Prize which would normally have been presented in January 1957. However because by then she would be in the USA the Queen Mother agreed to make the presentation six months earlier in July .

Five years after Ruth won the Field Services Scholarship one was also awarded to Jennifer Russell who spent a year in a High School in New York State before going on to University in Sheffield. In 1961 Ronessa Fisk won a Brooke Bond Travelling Scholarship which allowed her to spend sixteen weeks travelling in India before taking a degree in Fine Art at Durham University. During the Christmas holidays at the end of 1961 Diane Jaggs in the Lower Sixth attended an International Science Fortnight in London, the only girl from Norfolk and in August 1964 Janet Grief in the Lower Sixth was also selected to represent Norfolk at a similar event. She went on to study chemistry at York University (1965-68) and in 1966-67 was Captain of the University 1st XI hockey team. Susan Whitmore was chosen as one of only six representatives from Norfolk to attend the 10th International Youth Fortnight in 1968.

As at 'A' level the Ordinary Level results in 1954 were poor with a pass rate of only 61% and a mere 19% at grades 1 to 3. Out of the 56 fifth formers entered only 22 (39%) achieved five or more passes. By far the best results were in history with 36 passes out of 41 entries, 21 of them rated good. However only 37 pupils, and only 7 of them with good grades, passed English Language out of the 56 entered. Results in mathematics were even worse. Only 15 (6 of them with good grades) passed mathematics and only just over half the year group - 29 - were entered. Possibly jolted by these poor results they were very much better the following year with an overall pass rate of 75% of which 28% were grades 1 to 3; and some 60% achieved five or more passes. Another particularly poor year for 'O' level results was 1959 when the subject pass rate was only 60% (with 24% good). Less than 45% of the year group gained five or more passes. Miss Dore put this down to the fact that this was the first year when the three-form entry reached the fifth form.

The benchmark of five higher grade GCSEs, the equivalent of five 'O' Level passes is still used today. In the 1960s as in the previous decade the results varied from year to year. The low point was in 1960 when only 50% achieved five or more passes, albeit from an entry of 82, the highest number taking the examination to date. Although all the girls passed in at least one subject, many were said to be academically weak. The best results were in 1962 when 61 out of 82 students (74%) were successful and 1968 when 51 out of 72 (71%) achieved the benchmark figure. While ready to criticise if results were poor Miss Dore was also ready to give praise when results were good, as in 1966 when there was an 80% pass rate in biology, with 36 out of 74 girls achieving one of the top three grades. Miss Fish was warmly congratulated.

Pupil successes in competitions were not limited to those in the sixth form. In 1955 fourth-former Lesley Perry won first prize in an essay competition organised each year by the British Life Boat Institution and fifth-former Bridget McHale won the same prize in 1959.

The only HMI Report during Miss Dore's headship followed a four-day inspection in May 1950. Its conclusion was very positive in tone:

'The School is to be congratulated upon preserving its vital standards intact through a difficult period. It interprets its responsibilities widely and may justly take pride in its achievements. Problems lie ahead, principally in the academic field, but faced with the same spirit they will not defy solution.'

Miss Dore was praised as a 'resourceful and encouraging leader, well able to direct the forces at her disposal. Wise judgements and high standards characterise her leadership and the excellent personal relations prevailing in the school testify to her understanding of the individual.'

The inspectors acknowledged the major staffing problems, caused both by shortages and by illness, which the school had faced over the previous six years and the effect this had had. Furthermore over half the staff had joined within the previous two years. Despite these problems the staff were described as 'a loyal and co-operative team who set high standards of belief, conduct and industry to the girls.' They said that almost all were skilful and effective teachers and that two were outstanding. These two were not named in the report but clearly one of them was Miss Beardsell as shown by the following comment: 'The work in history is still in the hands of the sincere and gifted specialist who was appointed in 1919.'

Taking into account the staffing difficulties the general standard of work was found to be creditable. The English Department was however singled out as a cause for real concern; the direction of the work was described as 'timid, narrow and uninspiring'. The other major criticism was that attainment in many subjects was weakest at sixth-form level. There was 'generally need to develop in the girls a more mature approach to their work and to require a positive contribution from them; the poverty of their oral response is sometimes startling.' One criticism, which echoed one made in the previous report in 1933, was that there was 'a tendency towards over teaching noticeable in some departments' and this was seen as contributing to the problem of girls playing a less active part in their own learning than was seen to be desirable.

The inspectors were very complimentary about the corporate life of the school which they said was 'distinguished by sincerity, courtesy and enthusiasm.' They identified the morning Assembly as setting the tone which they said was maintained throughout the day by the personal example of the staff and the older girls. They also referred to the numerous societies which existed, supplemented by a variety of excursions such as those to concerts or bird sanctuaries and, in the holidays, by organised visits to other parts of England and to the Continent.

The premises were said to have both 'charm and dignity' but were recognised as 'inconvenient in many ways to a school of this size.' They pointed out that there were 10 forms but only 8 classrooms able to accommodate 30 girls. It was acknowledged that numerous skilful extensions and adaptations had been made to the buildings in the past, the most recent of which was the provision of a full-sized biology laboratory, which they said was having a beneficial effect on the work. While acknowledging that two small rooms would be released with the closure of the preparatory department it was felt that very little more adaptation was possible. They identified the need both for a specialist geography room and for the modernisation of the cookery room.

No doubt because of the damning report by HMI, the Head of English, Miss B Smith left in the summer of 1950. She had been at the school since 1929 and it was reported in the School Magazine that she was going to a boarding school near Basingstoke.

HMI clearly thought that the girls were well behaved and all the contributions I have had from former students confirms that this was the case. Shirley Bowler (Dexter), 1960-65, says that she 'enjoyed every moment there. All the teachers were so helpful and approachable….We would not have dreamed of swearing at them or misbehaving – had we done so we would have been in detention before you could say Miss Dore!' Nevertheless girls did occasionally break the rules and were punished as a result. Pauline Beeby (1947-54) remembers one winter when a small group of them were tempted the make snowballs with the clean snow on the Lower Garden. The inevitable result was a Wednesday afternoon detention during which they 'had to do sums involving £ s d in rows across and columns down.' Probably the most common punishments were for uniform infringements. According to Susan Stoakes (Hill) who was at the school from 1964 to 1971:

> 'A teacher always stood at the front door at 4 pm and checked that we had our berets and gloves on before we walked home and we were expected to keep these on all the way home even on the bus. Each bus was allocated a bus prefect whose job it was to ensure all berets were worn and we were well behaved. We used to cut up cereal boxes and put a strip inside our berets to make them stand up like pill boxes and pupils from Gaywood Park would steal our hats in the street and pull the green stalk out.'

Val Hawkins (Jaggs) recalls that it wasn't enough to wear the school beret; the badge had to be seen from the front. She also remembers the long queues outside Miss Dore's office in the winter when many girls had colds; sick notes from parents had to be seen personally by the Head Mistress when girls returned to school after being off ill. Miss Dore also saw girls for positive reasons, for example if someone gained three grade As for work in a particular subject then house points were gained and Miss Dore inspected the work before crediting the points.

The Old Girls' Association (OGA) was quickly re-established after the War with over a hundred members. In the next few years there were many well-attended social events including Halloween parties, Christmas parties, dinners, dances, sporting activities, theatre visits and amateur dramatics. But it is the nature of such organisations that support wanes after a time. Sadly in 1954 it was reported that the drama group, the badminton group and the keep-fit class had all closed due to lack of support, the Christmas party in December 1953 was attended by only a dozen members owing to a last-minute change of date and very bad weather and the dance in January had been a financial loss. 'The summer meeting was the final flop' as only a handful of people turned up. What a tale of woe!

However the Association was far from dead. At the annual dinner held in the school in 1955 the

Miss Dore, Miss Davis and the Prefects in 1960-61

guest speaker was Miss Clara Dow who captivated the audience with an account of her career, at the height of which she was principal soprano with the D' Oyly Carte Opera Company. Clara had been a pupil at the school over 50 years previously. For several years both the Christmas party and the annual dinner were well supported, for example in December 1955 there were about 100 at the party and in April 1956 some 70 attended the dinner at which Miss Green was one of the guest speakers. The other was Audrey Stratford who spoke about some unusual schools she had visited in Australia.

In 1954-55 a London branch of the OGA was formed which had a mailing list of 50 and an average attendance of 25 at each meeting that year. It continued to meet for several years. The last mention in the School Magazine refers to a meeting in December 1958 when a number of ex-pupils spoke about the school much earlier in the century. Edith Turner (1911-17) was even able to show the members a brooch which she had been given by Queen Alexandra. It was she who had written to the Queen's representative on the Governing Body to ask if the Queen's Prize could be presented personally at Sandringham. As a result this became the normal practice from January 1920.

After several successful years the OGA went through another bad patch and the 1960 dinner had to be cancelled because of a lack of support. It was decided that a different format should be tried and so the following summer an *American Open House* was held at which Miss Dore spoke about her trip to America. It was attended by about 40 people. In 1961- 62 the 75th anniversary celebrations already described were very well supported by Old Girls and at the September 1962

Miss Dore, Miss Fish and the Prefects 1964-65

AGM it was decided not to hold any events until the autumn of 1963 as it was felt there might not be enough support forthcoming. The pattern for the next few years was to hold an AGM and informal meal in the autumn and a summer meeting at the school which took various forms, for example a fashion show in June 1965 which was attended by about 100 people. At the summer meeting in 1966 a presentation of flowers and a cheque was made to Miss Davis on her retirement and it was later reported that she had bought a Suzy Cooper coffee set with the money.

Significant events were celebrated in 1967 and 1968. In April 1967 33 people attended a special luncheon in London to mark the school's 80th anniversary and the following year a social weekend on 28 and 29 June was held to mark Miss Dore's retirement. On the first evening the King Street site was open for people to tour the school. Coffee was served and photographs taken during Miss Dore's 24 years as Head Mistress were on display in the hall. The following day there was a coffee morning held at Queensway and a demonstration of modern educational dance was performed by girls from the third and fourth years. The highlight of the weekend was the dinner held in the Town Hall attended by over 100 people at which warm tributes were paid to Miss Dore and she was presented with a bouquet and a cheque. Diane Barrell (Jaggs), 1955-63, made a speech in which she pointed out that Miss Dore was an extraordinary person, someone who had a 1st class degree in history but had 'managed to combine an appreciation of the past with a very progressive attitude towards the present.'

Over the years the School Magazine was a wonderful source of information for alumnae. In each edition there were details of the comings and goings of large numbers of former students, including lists of marriages and births. In 1966, for example, the news section alone included information about some 70 people. It is a mark of the affection for and respect in which Miss Dore was held that she received such a huge number of letters and visits from which she provided the news about Old Girls. Large numbers of ex-students went into teaching and nursing but also into a wide range of other occupations, from cartographic draughtsman for the Local Government Commission (Barbara Pickett), to secretary for an aluminium company in Cincinnati, Ohio

Miss Fish and the sixth form 1966-67

(Elizabeth Martin), to give but two examples. Ann Ely (now Mrs Whitmore) who left school in 1958 trained as a bilingual secretary at the Lycée Francais de Londres where she won a prize for 'Travaux Practiques'. She wrote interesting letters to Miss Dore over several years about her work in France, in Geneva and in the USA. In 1961, for example, she was working as a translator for an aeronautical company in Geneva and sharing a flat with Pat Agar Strath who had also studied at the Lycée in London. The rent paid included the services of a maid who spoke both French and German. In one of her letters Ann strongly recommended that girls should seriously consider careers in languages because big organisations were crying out for those with such expertise.

Some memories of former students from this era have already been quoted but others are included below. Ruth Coulton (1945-56), writing in 1962 could still re-member catching the train for King's Lynn, aged 7, clutching a piece of bread and marmalade. Much later when she was in the sixth form she and one other travelled across town several times a week on very old bicycles to the Grammar School where they studied physics and chemistry. Perhaps surprisingly after so many years at the High School she said she was not nostalgic or sad on leaving. She was ready to move on. Margaret Lewis (1949-56), also writing in 1962 recalled being reported to Miss Dore for lateness: 'The subsequent interview was very painful, especially as instead of the anger I expected, I received a brief and reasonable discourse which made me feel silly and incompetent.'

Along with many former students, Janet Fendley (1963-70) very much admired Miss Dore whom she thought was an excellent Head Mistress. However she remembers with amusement her sex education lessons in which 'she said a lot of nothing and left us (or me) thinking 'What is she on about?' Basically the message seemed to be, 'Keep away from boys' and 'don't let 20 minutes of….(something) spoil your whole life'. It was all very vague.

Inevitably as numbers on roll went up so also did the teaching staff, from 18 in 1944 to 30 in 1968, including five men. Over the years as the school grew it experienced many problems in staff recruitment. In 1949, for example, Miss Dore reported that they were fully staffed for the first time since the War but this was not the case by any means in future years. Usually part-time staff, some of whom had retired, were used to cover the teaching. In 1960 there were as many as 13 part-time teachers. In addition, up to 1959, the Advanced level physics and chemistry were taught at the Grammar school because of the shortage of both well-qualified science staff and laboratory accommodation. Physical education was particularly hard hit by a frequent turn over of staff; in 1960 Miss Dore announced that 'for the first time we have been able to appoint two qualified physical training specialists.'

During Miss Dore's time as Head Mistress some long-serving staff retired. The first to go was Mrs T L Thomas who retired in December 1944 after being away ill for the first half of the Autumn Term. She was Senior Mistress for 16 years but had joined the school as a teacher of Mathematics in 1919. Miss E M Aylmer retired at Christmas 1950 having been on the permanent staff of the school since 1928. However like other long-serving staff she continued in a part-time capacity to help the school out following her official retirement. Miss G E Green retired in 1955 after more than 30 years at the school. A Cambridge graduate in Geography and Mathematics, she had joined the staff in 1924 and from that time had been in charge of the Geography Department. Miss Dore in an appreciation of her

Miss Dore and the Prefects in 1967-68

work in the School Magazine said, 'Many girls have reason to be thankful for her clear teaching and invigorating manner' and 'as the Derbyshire expeditions this year and last have shown, she can still out-walk and out-climb many teenagers. She will be much missed as a teacher and form mistress and for her general influence in the school.' In the event Miss Green continued to teach part time at the school for some four years after her official retirement.

Two years later Miss G M Hilditch retired after 32 years service. She joined the school in 1925, in 1941 became Head of French and in 1946 Senior Mistress. During the Spring Term of 1953, when Miss Dore was on leave of absence in the USA, Miss Hilditch was Acting Head and following that held the position of Deputy Head. An even longer-serving teacher left in 1958, Miss Emily Beardsell, who had been in Lynn some 41 years, the first two at the King Edward VII Grammar School. From 1919 she had been responsible for the History Department at the High School and from January 1945 to August 1946 was acting Senior Mistress, following the retirement of Mrs Thomas. We have seen that in 1950 HMI rated her highly. So also did the school. Miss Dore praised the fact that many girls had gone on to read history at university and many more owed to her their knowledge of local history. The 1958 Magazine also included a tribute by Dora Leonard:

'No one who was taught by her will fail to recognise her as a great teacher....Maybe the fact that I now read *The Manchester Guardian* relates back to her Currents Events Club meetings, so well worth staying for, even if a thirteen mile bus journey followed. In my mind's eye I can see her on break duty, with her characteristic walk, hands clasped in front of her, head a little forward, mind obviously busy, but nothing escaping her vigilant eye.'

In 1964 two long-serving staff retired, Miss Passmore and Miss Morris. Lesley Morris, who was in charge of Classics from 1949, had wanted to leave a year earlier but had stayed on because no suitable replacement could be found. This had proved a strain on her health and Miss Dore expressed the hope that with greater leisure she would enjoy greatly improved health.

Norah Passmore retired after eleven years as Head of the English Department. She was credited with greatly raising standards at both Ordinary and Advanced levels after the department had suffered severe criticism by HMI in 1950 and had continued to show poor results up to 1954. As a result of her teaching and leadership of the department many girls went on to read English at university and many more gained a life-long love of English literature. Her role both as producer of many successful school plays and in encouraging poetry reading and public speaking have already been mentioned. In addition her time-consuming but invaluable work on the School Magazine was praised by Miss Dore and warmly acknowledged in the 1964 Editorial.

Miss Dore in 1968

The Speech Competition continued after Miss Passmore's retirement. Carol Pike (Fenton) was presented with a copy of *The Complete Works of Shakespeare* for winning it in 1966 and went on to represent the school in a county competition at St Andrew's Hall in Norwich where the judge was John Laurie, a noted Shakespearian actor, although he became particularly known for his part as Private Frazer in *Dad's Army*.

As already mentioned, Miss Marian Davis retired in 1966. She had joined the school as Head of the Mathematics Department in 1948 and when Miss Hilditch left in 1957 she became Deputy Head. In the autumn term of 1960 she was Acting Head Mistress when Miss Dore had leave of absence to take part in lecture tour of the Canada and the USA. Somewhat unkindly she was known as 'cod face'.

Miss Dore herself retired in 1968. As we have seen, her contribution to the school was remarkable. In addition she played a very active part in the life of the town. Soon after her arrival in King's Lynn she was appointed a Justice of the Peace and later became Chairman of the Juvenile Court. She was the founder President of the local branch of the Business and Professional Women's Organisation, now sadly defunct, and in 1962-63 she was National Vice President. She was also for a time the Chairman of the King's Lynn Civic Society and a supporter of the Preservation Trust. On two occasions she was granted leave of absence from the school to allow her to travel to North America. In 1953 she was awarded a Walter Hines Page Scholarship offered by the English Speaking Union which enabled her to spend three months in the USA, principally to study the juvenile court system in the various states. In the autumn term of 1960 she went on a four month lecture tour to Canada and the United States on behalf of British American Associates, something she was invited to do again after her retirement. For two years from January 1969 she was Principal of the Anglican Training College for Women Teachers in Benin in Nigeria as part of the Voluntary Service Overseas programme. Miss Dore later described it as 'perhaps the most useful, certainly the most challenging, and definitely the most exhausting years of my life'. The college, for 250 resident students and 10 non-resident staff, was situated in a garrison town in a hot, wet, mosquito-ridden part of Nigeria!

In 1970 Miss Dore and her friend and fellow Head Mistress, Miss McGarry, retired to Tarrant Monkton near Blandford in Dorset. She led a very active life in retirement, for example as a lecturer and tour organiser for the National Trust. She travelled widely and wrote fascinating accounts of her experiences to friends and former colleagues. Miss Dore kept herself informed about the progress of the High School and visited King's Lynn on a number of occasions. One visit in particular should be mentioned. In 1994, she was invited to be present at the 40th anniversary celebrations of the Queen Mother's acceptance of the Freedom of the Borough of King's Lynn. Having attended the original ceremony in 1954 she was delighted to accept and turned up, aged 87, dressed very elegantly in a green and white, the High School colours. She died on 18 April 2004 aged 97.

Winifred Dore was an exceptionally able Head Mistress who really put the Girls' High School on the map. She would prove a very difficult act to follow.

5. 1968-77. An unrepentant believer in selection.

Miss Dore's successor was appointed in the Spring Term of 1968. Seven candidates were selected for interview and Miss Iris Sparkes, an honours graduate with a degree in French and the Deputy Head of Stowmarket Grammar School, was chosen. During the nine years she was at the High School the number of pupils rose from around 500 to 640.

Soon after her arrival Miss Sparkes informed the Governors that she would like to make a number of changes. In the curriculum she proposed to make French, mathematics and outdoor exercise compulsory for all fifth formers. She intended to give the sixth form 'slightly less freedom and some guidance' to ensure that the subjects studied were 'based on an informed choice.' She also wanted to change completely the arrangements made by Miss

Miss Iris Sparkes (EDP)

Dore for the use of the two sites. She suggested that Years 1 to 3 should be based at King Street and Years 4 to 6 at Queensway. She argued that this would give the seniors better access to recreational facilities and to more advanced and practical equipment. It would also reduce commuting as the juniors would not need to move to Queensway except once per week for games. Wednesday afternoon would cease to be lesson free as there would be no journeying to the playing fields and this would give greater flexibility in timetabling. She acknowledged that there were some disadvantages, such as the lack of small teaching spaces for sixth formers at Queensway and the lack of recreational space for the juniors at King Street. However she felt that the latter was more easily overcome than lack of access for senior girls. This re-organisation was approved by the Governors in March 1969 ready for the change to take place at the start of the autumn term.

Some girls were more affected than others by the decision to change the groups based at each site. Alison Childs (Howard), 1965-72, describes being at King Street for the first two years, at the new building at Queensway in the third year, back to King Street in the fourth year, then back again to Queensway in her last three years at the school.

By November of 1969 Miss Sparkes was pleased to be able to report to the Governors that the number of weekly bus journeys had been reduced from twenty-four to four during school hours. However she admitted that the changes had made the Queensway site overcrowded and that it might be necessary to have some sixth-form classes at King Street even though they would be based at Queensway. The old sixth-form common room at King Street had been converted into an excellent craft room but the modifications to the three laboratories which Miss Sparkes had requested to make them more suitable for junior forms had not been carried out. In fact the work was not completed until the end of 1970.

She also reported on the introduction of a new options system for the fourth and fifth forms. Everyone was to study English, mathematics and French and the other subjects had been grouped into five option pools. Certain restrictions had been imposed to prevent, for example, a girl choosing more than two practical subjects. In the third year Spanish was available as well as Latin with extra domestic science lessons for the less academically able.

Miss Sparkes also proposed changes to the school uniform. In February 1970 she told the governors that the school beret was no longer compulsory and that the special 'school' green would no longer be insisted upon. She believed that this would encourage more firms to stock the uniform and so help to keep prices down. Further relaxation followed in the autumn term of 1976 when she decided that uniform would be optional for sixth formers.

There continued to be accommodation problems for some years. From January 1970 the Corn Exchange was hired for games practices at lunchtime on one day each week. By the autumn term of 1972 all the fourth years were spending one morning at King Street doing chemistry and biology to relieve the pressure on the Queensway buldings. A year later two semi-detached houses, at 18 and 20 Queensway, were acquired by the local authority as a sixth-form centre but it took some eighteen months before they came into use. Lacks of funds delayed essential work, particularly the provision of central heating. It wasn't until after Easter 1975 that the sixth form started to use the new accommodation. By then all the furniture was in place and radiators had been installed but the work on the heating system was not completed until the autumn term and only after repeated telephone calls from the Head Mistress.

Pressure on accommodation at Queensway was made even worse in September 1976 when 104 pupils in the third year were transferred from King Street to replace fewer than 90 girls in the fifth year which had left. Miss Sparkes requested a mobile classroom but none was available.

Apart from the numbers of pupils other factors made the buildings uncomfortable. For example in the spring term of 1972 national strikes by coal miners caused widespread power cuts. Although the school did not close, parents' evenings were postponed until after Easter and after-school activities were curtailed. The school did become very cold but Miss Sparkes told Governors that, 'the girls were somewhat mollified by being allowed to wear boots in school all the time'.

Numbers on roll did vary during the 1970s. One worry was the loss of able fifth-form girls at age 16. Many more than in the past were deciding to study 'A' levels at the Norfolk College of Arts and Technology, as it was then called. This was first highlighted in the summer of 1974 and the following year Governors asked for a report on the situation.

Destinations of fifth formers 1970 to 1975

	A	B	C	D
1970	38	12	3	100
1971	23	5	1	93
1972	39	16	1	104
1973	37	17	5	86
1974	53	30	10	85
1975	50	32	15	79

The table gives the number of fifth-form leavers (A), the total number going to the College to study (B), the number going to the College to take 'A' levels (C) and the numbers in the High School sixth form are shown in (D).

By the mid 1970s NORCAT was able to offer twice as many subjects to 'A' level as the school and in modern and well-equipped accommodation. Statements such as, 'The laboratories, workshops and other practical facilities are among the finest in the country,' were heralded in an advertising campaign. The final straw for Miss Sparkes in what she saw as 'empire building' was a request by college staff in 1975 to go into school to speak to fifth formers about the courses on offer. Miss Sparkes reported to the Governors, 'This offer has not been accepted.' Of course today it is normal for school leavers to be given as much information as possible on the courses open to them so that they can make the most suitable choices. In the 1970s many schools felt threatened by the development of academic courses in colleges and feared that their sixth forms were at risk. This is well illustrated by a comment from Miss Sparkes in May 1976 when she referred to the fact that the college was continuing 'to sap our sixth form.' She was being pressurised by the local authority to reduce the cost of sixth-form staffing but that would have meant a reduction in the courses offered and led to even more girls wanting to study elsewhere.

There was no full inspection of the school during the 1970s. However an HMI survey of post-16 provision in King's Lynn and Downham Market was carried out during 1972-73 and a comment was made on the use of the Queensway site for sixth formers. The Report said that, although it seemed sensible, the building was not designed with the sixth form in mind and had several deficiencies, such as the lack of private-study accommodation and of teaching spaces for small groups, something Miss Sparkes had acknowledged when she first proposed the move. However other deficiencies were identified such as the inadequacies of the accommodation for biology, the lack of a base for religious education and the fact that some music lessons had to be taught in the dining room 'despite the unavoidable noise from the kitchen.' It was also pointed out that the use of the library for private study by the sixth form meant its use for other pupils was limited.

The report made interesting comparisons between sixth-form provision and outcomes in the High School compared with those at King Edward VII Grammar School, Downham Market Grammar School and NORCAT. One point made was that the High School had an open-access policy. If the Head Mistress and staff considered that a girl could benefit from being in the sixth form she was accepted and very few were denied entry. As well as Advanced level courses ones leading to 'AO' (Ordinary Alternative) and 'O' levels were also provided.

A major contrast with K.E.S. was in the destinations of students after the sixth form. For the two years 1971 and 1972 some 24 girls went to universities or polytechnics compared with 52 from K.E.S. and 37 girls went on to Colleges of Education compared with only 4 boys. The Report commented that an unusually high proportion of the girls looked towards colleges of education and teacher training and followed two 'A' level courses with other subjects to 'AO' or 'O' level. It said that, 'Few girls seem to be more than moderately ambitious academically and many remain at school beyond the age of 16 because their parents want them to rather than with firm examination objectives.'

The report contains little of the kind of detail on standards of work that appeared in previous HMI reports and few comments on staff. It said that the nature and quality of the teaching varied as in all schools but that there was much thorough and conscientious teaching and constructive individual help.

The school, 'despite its concern to establish higher academic achievement does not over-emphasise its 'A' level courses, and although one would expect more of the girls to want to take them, the success rate is very reasonable and shows signs of improvement.' The pass rate in 1971 was 68% and in 1972 82%; the average number of passes per pupil taking the examinations was 1.5 and 1.9 respectively. The latter statistics do illustrate clearly the point that most girls did not take three 'A' levels.

In conclusion the HMI said that, 'The school strives to meet the needs of all who wish to remain beyond 16. It challenges those seeking academic success and makes generous provision for others less ambitious.' The report's criticism is couched in mild terms:

> 'The genuine interest in study evident in the sixth form makes it difficult to understand the modest ambition of some girls and it may be that the latter cloaks traditional attitudes of the homes from which the girls come. It is regrettable if, because of this, some do not realise their full potential; but while respecting the girls' wishes the school pursues a policy of encouragement without undue pressure which is proving effective.'

In 1976 the school was subject to an informal HMI visit as part of a national survey of secondary school standards in core subjects. No official report was produced but on the basis of oral feedback Miss Sparkes informed the Governors that English was considered least good, science was pronounced very good and the mathematics department under Miss Bruce was outstanding. The inspectors had also told her that the deportment and appearance of the girls was 'quite exceptional'.

Obviously the girls did look smart in their school uniforms but in the 1970s it was perhaps even more unpopular then in previous decades. Nevertheless it would seem that rules were enforced just as firmly. Jane Massen remembers the girls being lined up each morning and a senior member of staff lifting their jumpers at the back to check that they were wearing the regulation tunics rather than skirts. A re-union was held in 1995 for girls at the High School from 1967-74 and a booklet was produced including people's memories of their time at school. Aspects of the uniform were mentioned by several people: 'Cycling to school trying to keep the beret on in case a teacher drove past' - Lois Cook (Hamon); 'Green socks. Yuk!' - Kathryn Priddin (Dean); 'The dreaded beret – Miss Morgan checking that we were wearing them, even on the bus home….

Doing PE in those awful pants' - Judith Waite (Horn); 'Green knickers' - Margaret Carter (McCabe); 'The revolting green of the uniform (remember those green knickers?)' - Pat Cooke Rogers (Cooke).

Many of the other memories were positive. Sadly one person commented that she 'hated school' and another said somewhat caustically that 'Anyone who says that school days are the best of your life has suffered from a seriously misspent adulthood.' Clearly there are people who have unhappy memories of their time at the High School but the overwhelming view from those who have contacted me is that it was a happy place and that their school days were good times. The reminiscences of Alexandra Kemp (Kampouropoulos) who was at the school from 1975 are particularly poignant:

'To a girl like me just out of an ordinary-looking primary school in Gaywood, the King Street buildings symbolised a remote, decayed antiquity and resonated with an air of antiquated mystery. I had never been or seen anywhere like it before. It was as if the rambling corridors, rooms and out-of-bounds areas treasured long-forgotten secrets they would not yield up till you got to know them well. It always felt as if the swaying banisters or the rickety staircase on the last flight of steps up to the Latin room at the top of the school might just give way, adding a hidden spice of danger to the mix. The art room with its shadowy rafters and inky easels just under the eaves at the other side of the quad looked the right setting for a ghost to appear.

I remember being entranced by the dramatic and powerful strains of Vivaldi's Gloria sung by the High School Choir sweeping out of the music room with its shining black grand piano, past the reproductions of Vermeer which hung outside on the first-floor which made you wonder about long-departed ages.

The teachers were inspiring, motivating and wanted the best for you. Mrs Middleton, the English and art and drama teacher, Mr Smart, the history teacher, and Mrs Riches and Mrs Lukey, who taught Latin, were phenomenal.

You had to work hard and you were pushed academically but there were plenty of opportunities for drama, charity organising and fundraising. In the first year, I was lucky enough to be chosen to play the Snow Queen in a production directed by Mrs Middleton. I wrote and acted in a play for the first-form drama competition, staged at lunchtime for charity. It was a spooky story about a haunted house, its owner and visitors and had to be no more than 3 minutes long. In the second year I took part in the High School's 90th birthday celebrations....

My favourite piece of work, an essay written in the fourth form, was an imaginary piece about being a suffragette. This was perhaps a seminal moment for me. Thirty years later I set up a local campaign to improve women's state pension rights and helped to draft Parliamentary amendments that changed the law in the Pensions Acts 2007 and 2008. It was King's Lynn High School for Girls that gave me the confidence and provided me with the underpinning skills to go out in the world to try and change things for the better....

I will never forget my days at the High School – one of the happiest times of my life.'

In the 1970s, perhaps because of the HMI Report mentioned above, more girls in the sixth form started to take three 'A' levels and go on the universities and polytechnics. Complete information on results and destinations is not available up to 1979. However the following table illustrates the trend:

Passes at 'A' Level:	4	3	2	1	Totals
1972	1	11	14	9	35
1973	0	13	21	13	47
1974	0	17	19	7	43
1975	0	17	10	7	34
1976	0	15	18	6	39
1977	0	19	10	6	35

The number of girls going on to universities and polytechnics rose from 10 in 1972 to 21 in 1975 and the number going to colleges of education fell from 16 to 4 in the same period. 1975 was a particularly successful year with a record eight students gaining Norfolk Scholar status, having been awarded at least two grade As or one A and two Bs at 'A' level. Rosemary Talbot and Catherine Robinson both gained three subjects all at grade A and Elizabeth Kleinerman, Aileen Odell, Alisa Rae and Jane Simmons gained three subjects with two of them at grade A. Rosemary, who gained the highest marks of any girl taking science subjects in Norfolk, was awarded an Open Scholarship in Medical Sciences at Girton College, Cambridge, Patricia Reynolds also got a place at Girton to read Natural Sciences and Catherine Robinson won a place at Hertford College, Oxford to read Medicine. It is not surprising that Miss Sparkes reported to the Governors that it was the school's best results to date.

Rosemary Talbot, who was also the Queen's Prize Winner for 1975, continued her success at

Rosemary Talbot, the 1975 Queen's Prize winner (LN)

Cambridge. In her third year she gained a 1st Class Honours degree and was awarded the Price University Scholarship worth £150 per year to continue her medical course at the London Hospital Medical School. She later became a leading paediatrician. Another university success came in 1977 when Lisa Hemeter who was in her first year at Leeds studying engineering was awarded an ICI Scholarship. She was one of only four women in a department of 130.

Results were also good in 1976 when two girls, Amanda Tealby and Susan Cross were both offered places at Sydney Sussex College, Cambridge. They were two of the first twenty-five girls ever to be admitted to the four-hundred-year-old College, which was one of only three former men's colleges to admit women that year. Amanda, who achieved 'A' grades in Latin, French and Spanish, won the prize awarded by Norfolk Education Committee for the girl gaining the highest marks in Arts subjects at GCE Advanced Level. Despite these successes however, the number going on to universities and polytechnics in 1976 fell back to 12 and the number going to colleges of education went up to 10.

At GSE Ordinary Level the highest number of students gaining five or more passes went up from 51 in 1969 to 80 in 1977. Unfortunately the percentage of the year group achieving the benchmark figure was not published and even Governors were only given percentage pass rates for each subject with no overall analysis. Miss Sparkes was not as open as her predecessor about examination results. However if one assumes that the number entered for English Language was the number in the year group then the percentage gaining at least five passes at 'O' level rose from 56% in 1969 to 83% in 1977, although neither the number nor percentage rose evenly:

Number of students gaining passes at GCE 'O' level:

	Cohort	9*	8	7	6	5	4	5+	%
1969	99	6	3	9	14	19	15	51	56
1970	86	16	7	11	10	10	10	54	63
1971	72	13	12	11	8	10	4	54	75
1972	95	15	17	12	10	12	6	66	70
1973	76	20	17	8	10	8	6	63	83
1974	99	28	12	11	10	0	10	61	62
1975	85	25	15	9	5	13	3	67	79
1976	93	36	12	11	12	8	7	79	85
1977	97	38	18	6	11	7	8	80	83

*or more

During the 1970's the Queen's Prize continued to be awarded each year for Service to the School by Queen Elizabeth, the Queen Mother. Like so many former students who later taught at the High School, the 1972 winner, Helen Carty (Horrex), has been Head of Geography at Springwood High School since 1993. She did a degree in geography and geology at the University of Sheffield and then went to Anguilla in the West Indies on VSO. She had planned to return home after two years but she got married and stayed for sixteen years. The 1976 winner, Susan Cross, was the third member of her family to win the Queen's Prize. Her grandmother (Mary Cross) was the prize winner in 1916 and her great aunt Ruth won the prize in 1913. Also in 1975 Susan's younger sister won the Queen's Bible, a prize awarded to a pupil at St George's School in Dersingham. As we saw above Susan was one of the first women students at Sydney Sussex

Helen Horrex with her parents and Miss Sparkes at Sandringham (LN)

Susan Cross, the 1976 Queen's Prize winner (LN)

College in Cambridge. A full list of all the Queen's Prize winners is provided in Appendix 1 and Appendix 2.

High School girls also achieved success in a variety of competitions and events in this period. In September 1969 it was reported that, out of an entry of 61000, Linda Wilkinson was one of three senior prize winners in a literary competition organised by *The Daily Mirror.* Her description of the Marshalsea Prison, made famous in *Little Dorrit* by Charles Dickens won her a prize of £50. Anne Watson in the Lower Sixth was chosen as one of Norfolk's six representatives at the International Science Fortnight in London in 1969. According to Miss Sparkes there was fierce competition for these places. Later that year Gillian Cooper and Beverley Smith won first prizes in the National Library Week Literary Competition. In 1971 more than 30 entries from the school reached the final stages in the National Children's Art Competition and both Susan Howard in the upper sixth and Isabel Isaacson in the fifth form had pictures exhibited at the Royal Academy. In 1973 and in 1975 the school came second in the Home Electrical Competition organised by the Electrical Association for Women and was awarded the Banbury Shield. Also in 1973 Abigail Braham, Yvonne Parks and Pat Woods won the local round of the public-speaking competition organised by the Business and Professional Women's Organisation and were runners up in the East Anglian final. In 1974-75 the High School team triumphed in a local competition, beating teams from the Grammar School and NORCAT to win the British Association of Young Scientists (BAYS) Cup. In the same year

The 1968-69 1st XI Hockey Team

The 1972-73 1st XI Hockey Team

Susan Featherstone won the Eastern Final of the White Fish Authority's Schools' Cookery Contest.

A rather different kind of award was made to third former Helen Moore. In January 1975 she was presented with a Royal Humane Society Certificate by the Mayor in recognition of her courage in rescuing a 12 year-old boy from the Middle Level Drain at Wiggenhall St Mary on 6 July 1974. Helen had jumped into the water to save the boy who had fallen fifteen feet from a bridge.

As in earlier years the School Magazine carried accounts of the many extra-curricular events and opportunities. It was to be produced in a new and slightly larger format from the summer of 1969 until 1976. The new cover was designed by Mary Ward and was said to be based on the theme of the new and old school buildings. In 1969 and 1970 the magazine carried editorials as in the past but this was replaced from 1971 by a forward written by the Head Mistress in which she commented on aspects of school life or on staff retirements. 1973 was the last numbered edition (no.47); those in 1974 and 1975 were shadows of former editions, consisting of duplicated sheets stapled into the new cover, presumably because of increasing costs and the small circulation. The final (50th) edition was produced in 1976, the same year as the High School Association was disbanded. This was a sad end for a publication that had been started in 1923 and had often run to thirty or more pages.

During the late 1960s and the 1970s a wide range of sporting opportunities was available.

Hockey and tennis continued to be the main sports but there was also netball, badminton, swimming and athletics, as well as gymnastic and modern dance clubs. In many of the sports there were several teams; in hockey, as well as the 1st XI and 2nd XI there were Under-15, Under-14 and Under-13 teams. Success in inter-school competitions varied from year to year and from sport to sport.

There were some good years for the school's hockey teams. In 1968-69 the 1st XI won the Fenland Tournament, came second in the Fenland League and reached the final rounds of the Norfolk Tournament. In 1972-73 the 1st XI, in a close finish, came second to Spalding High School in the Fenland League and won the newly donated silver cup at the Fenland Tournament which that year was held at Queensway. The 2nd XI also won their section of the Tournament. In 1974-75 the 1st XI only lost one of their eleven matches and came second in the Fenland League. Unfortunately they were unable to play in the Fenland Tournament that year. As in earlier years High School girls were selected to play at the County level, for example in 1970-71 Lesley Blackburn was a member of the Norfolk U18 1st XI as was Abigail Braham* in 1972-73. S Rybiczonek played in the Norfolk U15 1st XI the same year.

The best year for netball was 1974-75 when the 1st VII won all their friendly matches and were narrowly defeated (6-7) in the Norfolk Tournament. The U16, U14 and U13 teams also won most of their matches. Phillippa Medhurst and Karen Booth played regularly in the County 1st VII.

In athletics, following success in the town sports many girls each year went on to represent King's Lynn and District in the county championships. In 1971, for example, there were 10 Juniors, 15 Intermediates and 3 Seniors. Karen Booth finished 1st in the Junior Hurdles competition at Norwich and came 2nd in the Seven Counties Championships. The following year she reached the semi-finals of the All-England Championships. In the summer of 1973 she again represented Norfolk and the Seven Counties in the national competition and her time of 11.9 seconds in the 80 metre hurdles ranked her 12th in the country. Karen was voted King's Lynn Sportswoman of

the Year for 1973. Another outstanding athlete was Susan Attew who competed in the All-England Championships in 1973 and again in 1975, having broken the 20-year old record in the long jump at the school sports day.

In cross country three High School girls, unfortunately not named in the School Magazine, reached the national finals in 1969, as did Ruth Howes in 1970 and 1971. Unfortunately Ruth was unable to run in 1971 as she went down with appendicitis just before the event. Miss Sparkes sent her some flowers when she was in hospital. Ruth, shown in the photograph receiving the 1971 Prize for PE from Lord Wells-Pestell, recalls that all the prize winners had to remember to shake his left hand rather than his right. As

Karen Booth, 1973 King's Lynn and District Sportswoman of the Year (LN)

*Sadly Abigail was killed in a car accident on the A47 in 1976.

Head Girl she had to propose a vote of thanks and had to practise saying his name to ensure she did not make a mistake. From the late 1960s it was possible to use the hall at Queensway for Speech Days and this was a great improvement on the Corn Exchange.

The badminton teams had mixed fortunes over the years but hit the jackpot in 1973-74 when the 1st VI won the Norfolk Schools' Tournament. In the U19 competition Phillippa Medhurst won the Girls' Singles title and together with Wendy Smith the Girls' Doubles title. Karen Booth and her partner won the Mixed Doubles.

The school was regularly successful in the local swimming gala from which girls went on to represent the area at the Norfolk Gala in Norwich. In 1968 Mary Ann Robinson, went on to swim for the county, as did Susan Whiley in 1973. Susan came a very creditable second in the Division 8 Gala. The popularity of swimming lessons for the

Susan Attew breaking the school long jump record in 1975 (EDP)

Ruth Howes receiving the PE Prize in 1971

Speech Day at Queensway in 1972

first and second forms took a big leap in 1970-71 when the swimming pool was heated for the first time.

The gymnastics club was popular in this period and in 1972-73 there was even more enthusiastic participation, perhaps inspired by the performance of Olga Korbut and other Russian gymnasts in the Munich Olympics. In the Norfolk Schools' Olympic Gymnastic Championships in April of 1973 five girls took part at U13 level, four at U14 level and three in the U17 section. In the latter Linda Plowright, Caroline Black and Rosemary Talbot were placed 2nd, 3rd, and 4th respectively. The following year Jannette Burgess was placed 3rd in the Senior team event and Linda Plowright was 4th.

Tennis teams seemed to have less competitive success than girls in some of the other sports but in 1976 the U14 team won its section of the Fenland League Tournament for the first time ever. The outstanding tennis player in this period was Ruth Eakins, who was selected to play for a Great Britain U-14 tennis team in Paris.

As in previous years the annual programme of trips and visits did much to extend the horizons of the High School girls. Many were school-subject related such as the history trips to the Iceni Village for the first form, to Castle Acre for second years and to Norwich Cathedral and Museum for third years. Other popular trips were to the London Planetarium, Madame Tussauds and the Science Museum for the fifth form, the sixth-form geography field courses to North Wales or Dorset, visits to the National Gallery, trips to hockey international matches at Wembley, exchange visits to France and Spain and the many theatre trips to London, Stratford, Cambridge, Peterborough, Norwich, Ipswich and Bury St Edmunds. One theatre trip worthy of mention was that to see *Antigone* by Sophocles at King's College in London. A leading role in that production was played by Carolyne Ballard who had been in the sixth form at the High School the previous year and had gone up to King's to read Classics. There were also trips to special events such as the Tomorrow's World Exhibition in London in 1974 and to see the Thracian Treasures at the British Museum or the 1776 Exhibition at Greenwich, both in 1976. With the introduction of the Duke of Edinburgh Scheme in 1970-71, groups working towards the Gold Award took part in a number of expeditions such as that to Llangollen in 1971.

The traditional fourth-form trip in this period became essentially a geography field course to Derbyshire, although it did include other elements such as a visit to the Wedgewood factory in the Potteries or to stately homes such as Chatsworth House. Miss Dore's departure meant that the Stratford element of the trip had been lost.

As well as the school exchanges there were a number of other foreign trips such as those to Paris and Austria (to ski) in 1971 and France and Belgium in 1973. At Easter 1975 Miss Hampson, Miss Breeeze and Mrs Gilbert took a party of 30 girls on the *SS Uganda* which sailed to the Eastern Mediterranean. From the account in the School Magazine it was obviously a splendid trip but I was surprised to read that they had crossed the 'Baltic' Sea to reach Trabzon in northern Turkey! In December 1976, 35 girls took part in another British India cruise and spent a magical Christmas in the Holy Land. One particularly unusual trip was that to the decennial passion play at Oberammergau in Germany in 1970. Unfortunately the School Magazine contains no account.

During this period members of the sixth form attended a number of educational conferences. Some were specifically aimed at students wishing to study particular subjects at university such as mathematics, physics, chemistry or engineering. Others had somewhat broader aims such as Schools' Christian Fellowship training courses and Challenge of Industry Conferences. Several years running a number of High School girls joined groups of Norfolk students who attended the British Association for the Advancement of Science (BAAS) meetings, for example at Exeter in 1969, Durham in 1970 and Swansea in 1971. In 1973 eight girls went to the British Association of Young Scientists (BAYS) 'Science is Fun' Conference at Huddersfield Polytechnic. By 1974 the Local Authority had decided to restrict the number attending the BAAS conference to one delegate per school and Catherine Robinson was chosen to go to the University of Sterling as part of the Norfolk delegation. Her article in the 1975 School Magazine concludes:

'It was certainly an intellectually stimulating experience and not only during the daytime. I can recall a fellow member of the party trying to make me visualise the fourth dimension ('Once you have got the fourth, the fifth is easy') at an early hour of the morning. I am left with a jumble of assorted memories: someone's amazement that the tea party for chemists really was a tea party; my first experience of quadraphonic sound; the chairman of the Brains Trust diplomatically seating Magnus Pike at the end of the panel so he could not hit Sir Bernard Lovell while he was gesticulating in answering a question; and not least the mass of data I accumulated during the week.'

Under the guidance of Miss Violet Chilleystone, who had joined the staff in September 1967, music flourished, despite the problems posed by the split site. She was responsible for a series of successful productions based on famous operas, beginning with *Pagageno* in 1969, staged in the new hall at Queensway. This was followed by *Hansel and Gretal* in 1970, *Turkish Delight* in 1971, *The Bride of Seville* in 1972, and *The Marble Guest* in 1973. Usually the operas were

The Bride of Seville, 1972 (EDP)

performed on two nights in May and the entertainment also included an orchestral concert. Some 300 girls were involved in the combined concert and opera in 1971. By 1972 the school orchestra, under Mr Peace and Mr Bentley, included over 70 instrumentalists and could be supplemented by a large number of recorder players.

1971 saw the 25th anniversary of the first of a series of lunchtime concerts, held originally at the Town Hall and later at the Guildhall, which over the years many High School girls had been able to attend and appreciate the talent of both well-known and up-and-coming musicians. In 1971 for example they included 'three youthful artists from the Yehudi Menuhin School', one of whom was Nigel Kennedy aged 13 years. At the 25th anniversary concert itself a piano and oboe recital was given by Lady Fermoy and Lady Barbirolli. The following year one of the concerts featured the King's Singers, a consort of former choral scholars from King's College in Cambridge, and a group still in existence to day although including none of the original members. Sometimes the girls would be allowed to turn the pages of the music score for pianists and Jean Holland (Howes) remembers doing that for Richard Rodney Bennett and for John Lill, although that was in the late 1960s.

It was under Mr Roy Whittingham, Head of Music from 1975, that music really took off. Two large-scale concerts were held in 1975-76. That at St Margaret's at Christmas was said to be so successful that a repeat performance was held at Hillington Church to raise money for the Scnetzler organ appeal. At the King's Lynn Festival in the summer of 1977 *The Fall of Jericho*, written and composed by Mr Whittingham, was performed by 150 instrumentalist, singers and dancers in St Nicholas Chapel to great critical acclaim. Christopher Hogwood described it as 'one of the highlights of the Festival'.

Straight drama in the 1970s had a lower profile. In 1971 there was a joint production with the

A 1920s jazz band, part of the 90th birthday celebrations, 1976 (LN)

Grammar School of *Under Milk Wood* by Dylan Thomas. This was to be the last such venture. However dance-drama was popular and a number of performances were staged at Queensway. As part of the 90th anniversary celebrations in November 1976 a light-hearted review devised by Mrs Lewis and Mr Whittingham was staged on two nights. Different playlets were put on representing each decade of the school's life. Alex Kemp (Kampouropoulous) took part in a Speech Day in the Edwardian era: 'I was on the stage all by myself for this in front of the whole school - quite scary - to give a recitation, dressed up in a navy sailor's dress with red ribbons.' Other acts included the Beatles hit *There goes my Baby* in the 1960s slot and a 1920s jazz band. As part of the celebrations Miss Sparkes organised an exhibition of photographs and documents from the school archive.

In the 1970s the most popular societies, perhaps inevitably, were those which involved both girls and boys but not all survived until re-organisation. Attempts to hold fortnightly meetings of the Inter-Sixth Society in 1971-72 were thwarted by power cuts but they did manage to hold a varied programme nevertheless. The Inter-Sixth is not mentioned after 1973 but the History Society with its programmes of trips, lectures, debates and discussions was still flourishing in 1976. In 1969-70, for example, the meetings included a stimulating discussion on the Arab-Israeli conflict which was 'totally dominated by the boys'. Other groups which were active for several years were the Geography Society, the Arts Society, the Science Society and the Christian Union. In 1973 a branch of BAYS was started in West Norfolk and was active for three years but later in the 1970s the nearest branch meetings were in Norwich.

For the younger pupils a variety of clubs was often organised by sixth formers. These varied from year to year but included ones for drama, stamp collecting, art and craft, natural history, netball, hockey and chess. The Local Knowledge Club was still active in the 1970s and, as

The 90th anniversary exhibition (EDP)

mentioned above, the Gym Club was well supported in this period.

Maintaining the long-standing tradition of raising money for charity, over £300 was donated to Shelter in 1969. Complete information is not available for all years but in 1972, for example, £300 was contributed to the St Raphael Club in Gaywood, in the autumn term of 1973 £100 was donated to the Samaritans and the following year a further £250 was donated, having been raised by a non-uniform day, a waste-paper collection and a May Fair organised by the sixth form. In the autumn of 1975 £200 was raised for Leukaemia Research and Guide Dogs for the Blind. And every year the sixth form took the produce from the Harvest Festival to an Old Folks' Club as they had done in the past.

Unfortunately by the mid-1970s the Old Girls' Association had been disbanded. It would never be the same once Miss Dore's enthusiastic interest and support were lost. Although 56 attended a wine and cheese party in the summer of 1969, the AGM and dinner, which was to have been held at the Riverside Rooms the following September, had to be cancelled through lack of support. A wine and paté party with entertainment provided by Anne Pratt and Angela Rose was held at Queensway in January 1970 but only 17 attended due to bad weather and a flu epidemic. At the AGM held in April there were only six members. It was at this meeting that Miss Sparkes suggested that the name should be changed from the Old Girls' Association to the King's Lynn High School Association. However a name change was not enough to halt the decline.

A successful car rally was held each year from 1970 to 1975 but other events were less well supported and in 1971 the Association had only 37 members. The AGM in October 1971 was reasonably well attended as the guest of honour was Miss Dore who spoke about life in Africa. Some 36 members were there to hear her speak. It is a significant that, apart from the usual lists of births and marriages, the 1972 edition of the Magazine contained news of only four former students.

In September 1974 an extra-ordinary general meeting was held to discuss the question of the future of the Association in the face of dwindling support. Although only a small number was present, the general view was that the Association should continue and so three social events were organised that year including the annual car rally. However attendance varied and the Secretary, Lesley Thain, commented in the 1975 Magazine: 'the difficulty remains of finding sufficient support among the relatively few Old Girls who still live in the area.' When the Governors met in November 1975 Miss Sparkes reported with regret the demise of the High School Association. From the funds £80 had been donated to the school to provide an annual prize of £5 for mathematics. In May of 1977 it was revealed that the disbanded association also had a Jubilee Fund totalling some £666.74. It was decided that the money should be used to make grants towards the cost of the expenses incurred by girls attending for interview at higher and further education institutions.

In the 1970s two former members of staff made gifts to the school. In May 1971 Miss Sparkes reported to the governors that Mrs Beatrice Dorer, who retired in December 1938 after 20 years as the classics mistress, had left a picture by the local artist Walter Dexter to the school. She said that she had accepted it on the understanding that if the school ever closed it would be returned to the Dorer family. This was the High School's second Dexter as one had been donated by the Miss Tizzard, Art Mistress from 1925 to 1942.

In 1974 the former Head Mistress, Miss Rose Williamson, wrote to Miss Sparkes to say that she would like to give the school a sum of money and it was decided to use it to enhance the appearance of the grounds at Queensway. Lack of funds meant that part of the original plans for the site, which had included the planting of shrubs in the quadrangle and trees to form an arboretum, were axed. In an effort to make the site less bleak, former students contributed to the purchase of roses, parents sent cuttings from their gardens and some trees were bought or donated. Miss Williamson's gift was used to complete the planting of the arboretum in a much more interesting and colourful way than had been originally planned.

In addition Miss Williamson made a gift of £100 to endow a prize to be known as the E D Drever Prize for Music. Miss Drever had taught music and eurhythmics at the school from 1928 to 1941. Preference was to be given to students intending to make a career in the teaching of music. The cousins had made a home together after their retirement, and although they never visited the school they did keep in touch and welcomed former staff and old girls who went to see them.

A number of staff who had been at the school for a very long time retired during the 1970s, notably Miss Phyllis Brown who had been a pupil at the school and was in the first instance taken on to help in the kindergarten after completing her Higher School Certificate in 1926. She eventually was put in charge of the preparatory department and when it finally closed in 1952 Miss Brown was kept on as a junior form mistress and to teach needlework in the senior school. The 1950 HMI Report was very positive about the preparatory department saying that the work was 'enlightened and that the girls enjoyed it. The Mistress in charge....has given 24 years faithful service in this post and may well take pride in this record.' Her expertise with the juniors was recognised in 1969 when she was made Head of Lower School. She retired in 1971 after 45 years on the staff and Miss Sparkes was fulsome in her praise, saying that it would be difficult to imagine King Street without her. She had coped 'quickly and efficiently with the crises of school life, encouraging the apprehensive, re-assuring anxious parents, helping new staff to find their way.' She said that mothers bringing their eleven-year-old daughters were pleased to see her as they themselves could often be numbered among her old pupils.

One of the first men to hold a senior post at the school, Richard Lee, retired in 1972 after twelve years, for the most part as Head of English. Miss Sparkes tribute was extraordinary:

'Modest and unassuming by nature, Mr Lee, like all good things, grows upon one slowly; one comes to recognise and to appreciate a tolerance, a generosity of spirit, which finds good in all. Perhaps the rarefied air which he inhabits encourages a certain Olympian detachment towards the quirks and oddities of lesser mortals. Certainly he walks more freely in the visionary world of his beloved Blake but one notices that he brings back from the company of the immortals a shrewdness of judgement, an insight into character, which makes his estimate of the girls he has taught not the least valuable part of his work as a sixth form master.'

Mr Lee is remembered by former students as a quiet, gentle and lovely man but one who was not a strong disciplinarian. One person who was at the school from 1965-72 recalls that when she was in the fifth form he regularly sent groups out into the corridor. They would nip out of school to buy a drink and be back for the end of the lesson. 'We ran rings round the poor man. Looking back I feel ashamed.' Another memory was of Mr Lee being persuaded that all they needed to know about Shaw's *Pygmalian* could be gleaned from listening to songs from *My Fair Lady*. From the account several lessons were spent in this way. Perhaps these memories explain the somewhat barbed comments in Miss Sparkes's retirement tribute.

It must have been somewhat difficult for male teachers and history teacher Mr Smart wrote an amusing article in the 1973 magazine entitled *One man went to school*, in which he identified the following reactions on finding himself in a woman's world for the first time: sudden terror, delight, some sadness, bewilderment, occasional regret, gratitude, anger, frustration, satisfaction and enjoyment. Each of these feelings was illustrated with examples such as his anger at seeing the slogan 'Down with male chauvinist pigs' and then on being told, 'We didn't mean you, Mr Smart - we don't think of you as a man'!

In 1975 Miss Violet Chilleystone retired as Head of Music. Her strong contribution to extra-curricular music has already been mentioned. Although she had only been on the staff for eight years her association with the High School went back a very long way. She was an old girl of the school who left in 1929, after taking her HSC, to train as a teacher of music and she taught for 45 years in total, mostly in London. She was clearly highly regarded by Miss Sparkes who said: 'I do not think I have ever met a more dedicated teacher or one who showed more pleasure when asked to accomplish the impossible.' One former student has described Miss Chilleystone as 'an absolute sweetie.' She was 'very short and round, with her hair platted into an earphone over each ear. She always seemed very smiley and bouncy and reminded me of the little lady in *The Sound of Music* who kept bowing at the end of the film.' Another former student, Julie Dixon (Bunting) says: 'She may have been only four feet tall, but she was scary with it' and, with reference to yet another film, points out that her hair style was one 'later popularised by Princess Leia in *Star Wars.*'

Some teachers who are remembered fondly and/or with respect by former students have already been mentioned, for example by Alex Kampouropoulos. Others include Miss Brand, Miss Breeze, Miss Cade, Mrs Campbell, Miss Chester, Miss Fish, Miss Fraymouth, Mrs Gridley, Mr Growcott, Miss Hampson, Mrs Hardwick, Mr Kennett, Mrs Mann, Miss Morgan, Mrs Perryman, Miss Readwin, Mr Scorah, Miss P Smith, and Mr Tallack to list just a few. However there are almost certainly others who deserve to be mentioned.

The teacher mentioned more than any other was Mrs Hardwick, now Dr Back. For Stephanie Reeve (Lovick), she was a 'brilliant English teacher who actually made stuff interesting and to this day makes me picky about grammar and spelling.' Suzanne Everington (Day) agrees with the latter sentiment and laments, 'If only children were taught that way today.' Susan Wilkin (Hansen) also agrees that 'Mrs Hardwick was a brilliant English teacher although very scary!' She made the books of Charles Dickens come alive for Susan. Diane Gardiner (Henson) expresses her thanks to Mrs Hardwick who she says 'had a wicked sense of humour and boy did she get us to have a good work ethic.' For Linda Ashby (Gillies), 'Mrs Hardwick was strict.... but she was an excellent teacher.' Rosie Paul says that Mrs Hardwick 'helped to make me who I am.' Jane Ford (Bradshaw) sums it up by saying, 'For me, like many others, it was Mrs Harwick [who really made a difference]. I became a teacher and often think of how inspirational she was.'

A major area of concern for governors, staff, pupils and parents of the High School in the 1970s was the proposals for the reorganisation of secondary education in the King's Lynn district. The first proposal put forward by the Western Area Divisional Executive in May 1971 was for K.E.S. to become a post-16 centre and the other schools to be 11-16 comprehensives. As one might expect both the staff and the Governors at the High School were against this idea and even at K.E.S. the teachers were divided, some wanting it to be a 14-18 school rather than an institution solely for post-16 students. By 1975 it was clear that the local authority planned to move to a system of 11-18 and 11-16 mixed-sex and all-ability schools in West Norfolk. Public notices were published to create 11-16 schools in Hunstanton and West Walton in the summer of 1975 and it was announced that as from I January 1976 the two separate Alderman Catleugh schools - for Boys and for Girls – would be brought under one Head, in preparation for the re-organisation that was to come in King's Lynn. The person appointed was Miss Norah Howe-Smith, herself an old girl of the High School.

The High School Governors discussed the pros and cons of various options for King's Lynn in December 1976 and it was at this meeting that Miss Sparkes announced her resignation, to take effect at the end of the following summer term. The local authority's favoured option was the creation of three 11-18 schools: King Edward VII High School; Gaywood Park High School and a school formed by the amalgamation of the Girls' High School and Alderman Catleugh School. By the summer of 1977 this was the firm proposal. At a meeting held in May officers from the local authority met the Governors to discuss the transfer of the High School premises in King Street and at Queensway to Norfolk County Council on a leasehold basis should the formal re-organisation proposals be approved. In that event a scheme would be agreed with the Charity Commission whereby the assets of the High School would be held in trust for the benefit of girls in the area.

Like her predecessor, but not to the same extent, Miss Sparkes was involved in the local community. She was a founder member and first Secretary of the King's Lynn Soroptomists. She was a person of strong opinions and even one of her professional referees when she applied for the headship commented that she did not suffer fools gladly. It has been said that she knew what she wanted and achieved it by excellent organisation. Her letters, which were brief, courteous and lucid, were said to be characteristic. She was also a good public speaker. On the personal side she could be very charming and was a lively and amusing companion. She was particularly fond of her cats.

Miss Sparkes was wary of so called experts in education. At the 1970 Prize Giving she said that, 'We live in an age of the expert. But educational experts come and go. It is the teachers who are really going to influence the quality of education.' She returned to this theme at a similar occasion in 1974:

'I do not think it unfair to say that there is not an adult in this room who does not consider himself an expert in the field of education. There is some foundation for this. We have all been processed by the system, some more intensively than others. But with this proliferation of experts has come a proliferation of ideas: some good; some completely unworkable; and some lunatic. One longs for sanity and quiet appraisal of values that are truly educational.'

She often did not see eye to eye with local authority officers and especially advisers who were not made welcome at the School.

An article in *The Times Educational Supplement* about the High School reported that 'the Head is politely but firmly the boss of the show…there is no parent-teacher association as she thinks they fall into three types: interfering, social or fund-raising. She is always willing to see parents but they must leave education to the professionals.' According to one informant she did not

The prefects in 1970-71

The prefects in 1972-73

relish parents' evenings and on one occasion, when she felt that the consultations with staff had gone on too long, she is reported to have asked parents to leave telling them that she and the caretaker needed to get to bed! This makes a good story even though it may be apocryphal.

Views on Miss Sparkes by former students are mixed. She was certainly not regarded by everyone as highly as was her predecessor. Some former students have said that they found her more remote than Miss Dore and felt that she showed less interest in them as individuals. Is it significant that she was not photographed with the prefects or the sixth form?

However Sue Stoakes (Hill) saw a very different side of Miss Sparkes.   When she discovered that Sue's abusive father was insisting that she left school at 16, she invited Sue to stay in her flat for the time she was in the sixth form, applied for grants for her and finally saw her safely off to a teacher-training college in Leicester. On her 18th birthday Miss Sparkes and Miss Morgan gave her £10 to take some friends out for dinner at The Duke's Head. Sue, who retired in 2011 after 35 year teaching mathematics, has very happy memories of Miss Sparkes who she says showed her nothing but 'extreme kindness and affection.'

Another former student who says that she was very strict but had a soft side, remembers her as 'a great teacher of Latin….She once fell off her desk during a particularly animated Latin lesson, but carried on teaching from the floor which gained her the respect and affection of everyone present.' She obviously had a sense of humour and caused much amusement in an assembly when she was given a tapestry frame as a leaving present. She joked that she would remember the girls when she stabbed the needle in and out of the tapestry!

Miss Sparkes was completely against the proposals for comprehensive re-organisation in King's Lynn. In an interview with the local press, when she announced that she was to leave in 1977 to become Head of Derby High School for Girls, she said, 'I am an unrepentant believer in schools of this type. Only a philistine would wish to preside over the abolition of a fine school like this.' She left her headship post in Derby in 1982 and set up an antiquarian book business.

6. 1977-79. The end game.

For the final two years before the High School closed Miss M H Morgan was Acting Head Mistress. She had joined the school as Deputy Head in 1966 from Cathays High School in Cardiff where she had been Head of the English Department. Her two years in charge until her retirement in the summer of 1979 could not have been easy. A selective girls' school of over 650 was due to close and to be merged with a secondary modern school to form a much bigger unit of some 2000 all-ability girls and boys. A great deal of planning and preparation would have to take place in addition to the normal day-to-day running of the split-site school.

Yet normal life did go on. Visits took place, clubs and societies met and musical and drama productions were staged. The school's final dramatic production was *A Midsummer Night's Dream* produced by Mrs Lewis in the spring of 1979. There were the usual trips to theatres, museums and galleries, history and geography trips, French exchanges, ski trips and, for the first

Miss Mary Morgan

time, music tours. Following the success of *The Fall of Jericho* in the 1977 King's Lynn Festival, which was seen by a party of Germans from Trier in the Moselle Valley, Roy Whittingham was invited to take the school orchestra on its first foreign tour. Some 45 members of the orchestra and singers spent five days in November in Trier where they gave three concerts. It is said that they were not in the least disconcerted at playing Beethoven to a discerning German audience. In the summer of 1979 the choir went on a tour to Bavaria and Austria. Earlier that year, at the spring half-term, Miss Russell and Mrs Gold took a party skiing to the Italian Alps.

Sixth formers had the opportunity to attend a number of conferences such as those for historians and for linguists at the University of East Anglia in 1979. There was a good attendance of High School girls at the monthly BAYS lectures in Norwich and two students were selected to attend the British Association for the Advancement of Science meeting at Bath in the autumn of 1978.

Over the years the school had an excellent record of encouraging the girls to have a social conscience with respect to those less fortunate than themselves and this continued to the end. In the summer of 1978 some £760 raised by various means was divided equally between the Imperial Cancer Research Fund and the West Lynn Children's Home. In the autumn term the school orchestra took part in a concert arranged by the Lions Club and some £200 was raised for the Marsh Lane Hydrotherapy Pool Fund. The following spring over £1000 was donated to the Multiple Sclerosis Association and a local school for handicapped children. As in previous years the produce taken to the Harvest Festival was distributed to members of an Old Folks' Club. In

Part of the orchestra rehearsing before their trip to Germany in 1977 (LN)

the autumn of 1978 that amounted to over 100 carrier bags.

As if the problems of keeping the school running normally in those last two years were not enough, Miss Morgan had to deal with a number of major problems. One was union action. In the Spring of 1978 members of the National Union of Teachers and of the National Association of Schoolmasters/Union of Women Teachers caused major disruption in many schools. The High School did not close but as a consequence of the ban on lunchtime supervision Miss Morgan and the Acting Deputy Head, Miss Hampson, had to provide all staff cover over the lunch break for the last eight days of the term.

1979 saw a string of problems. Firstly a strike on the railways caused a shortage of fuel at Queensway towards the end of January and the building had to be closed. Miss Morgan thought that it was better to disrupt the education of the Lower School so those in the first, second and third forms were sent home at the close of school on Tuesday 23 January and the senior forms were transferred to King Street. An emergency delivery of oil at the weekend meant that normal school was resumed the following week. Secondly a blizzard on the Friday before the spring half-term caused the school to be closed for the day and only 200 girls and 16 staff had been able to get to either of the two school sites on the previous day.

The worst problem was caused by a fire which broke out on the night of 22-23 March 1979 at King Street and, despite prompt action by the Fire Brigade, damaged the physics laboratory, the art room and three store rooms. In addition two form rooms underneath those damaged by fire were put out of use by water damage. The school had to be closed but only for four days. It was possible to transfer most of the art classes to the craft room but physics groups had to share the biology laboratory on alternate weeks.

Some of the fire damage at King Street in March 1979 (LN)

In the Autumn Term of 1976 the Public Notice setting out the re-organisation proposals in the King's Lynn area had been published. At this stage the name of the new High School which would be formed by the amalgamation of the Girls' High School and the Alderman Catleugh School had not been settled. After the re-organisation, the King Street premises would continue to be used although it was hoped that this would not be a long-term measure. In fact it was envisaged that they might be taken over by K.E.S. from September 1981 or 1982, although this plan was later abandoned. The proposals listed the partner-primary schools for each of the three new schools in King's Lynn and the aim was to provide a roughly equal share of the different socio-economic areas in the town and surrounding villages, so that as far as possible the three secondary schools would each have the chance to develop a fully comprehensive intake. Children at the 11-16 schools in Hunstanton, West Walton and Terrington would be able to transfer to any of the three Lynn schools or to NORCAT for post-16 education. The local authority's re-organisation scheme was finally approved by the Department of Education and Science in the spring of 1978.

Preparations for re-organisation took a number of forms. Training was organised to help staff prepare for teaching children of all abilities, although many staff did not relish the changes and some took the option to retire or found posts in other schools. The Head of Mathematics, Miss Winifred Bruce, left in the summer of 1978 to take up a post at Dame Alice Harpur School in Bedford. Mr Roy Whittingham who left in 1979 was also lost to the independent sector.

In July 1978 a joint meeting of the Governors of the High School and Alderman Catleugh School was held at which Miss Morgan and Miss Howe-Smith set out the proposed staffing structure

Rosemary Eakins presents a bouquet to Miss Morgan at the school's last Speech Day in 1978 (EDP)

for the new school. At the same meeting possible names for the new school were considered. These included Alderman Catleugh High School, Queen Elizabeth ll High School, Queensway High School and Queens* High School. No decision was taken but it was agreed that the name should be the first item on the agenda for the Shadow Governing Body which was to be set up. In the meantime the views of staff would be canvassed. When the meeting took place in September it was agreed that the name of the new school would be none of the ones suggested above but Springwood High School. The Head Master Designate of the new school, Mr M W Griffiths, appointed by a joint committee in the summer term, was present at the meeting. Arrangements were made for the appointment of other staff to posts of responsibility. In the event many of the Heads of Department posts went to High School staff and most of the pastoral posts to teachers from Alderman Catleugh School. There were also appointments from outside the two schools.

There were many loose ends to tie up as far as the High School was concerned. For example at a meeting of the Governors in May of 1979 it was decided that all the school's pictures, most of them prints of old masters, but including the Dexter donated many years previously by Miss Tizzard and possibly that left to the school in 1971 by Mrs Dorer, were to be passed on to Springwood High School, along with all the silver trophies which were re-assessed for insurance purposes.

Mary Morgan retired in the summer of 1979 when the High School closed. She had served the school well as an efficient deputy head for over ten years before being thrown into the job as Acting Head. It is much to her credit that things as went as well as they did. According to Julie

* The Governors' Minute does not show an apostrophe. Presumably it could have been either Queen's High School or Queens' High School had that name been chosen.

*Several views of
Old School Court
(M Walker)*

Bunting, 'She could silence a whole hall just by looking over her glasses' and 'had great presence.' She was also a highly-regarded teacher of English.

This was not however the end of the story. The High School girls became pupils of Springwood High School in September 1979 and many of them went on to be very successful academically, in music, in drama, in sport and in a range of other activities. Springwood High School today is a popular and well respected comprehensive school but its history must be left for another book. However I can perhaps be permitted to mention one person who achieved outstanding success in sport. Kathy Johnson (Edwards) competed in three Olympic Games as a member of the GB Hockey team and won a Bronze Medal at the 1992 Olympics in Barcelona. She was also a Gold Medallist at the European Nations' Cup in Brussels in 1991. Kathy was only at the Girls' High School in its last year but it can still claim some reflected glory.

The assets of the High School were vested in a charitable trust. As already mentioned the King Street building was sold in 1985 (for a sum of £150,000) and converted into the modern apartments of Old School Court. Up to the summer of 1985 the buildings were used by Springwood High School and an annual rent of £6000 from 1 September 1979 was paid by the local authority. They also paid a rent of £750 per year for use of the land owned by the Trust at Queensway. The Charity Commission Scheme, sealed in June 1983, listed five nominative trustees (one appointed by The Queen, two by Norfolk County Council, one by the Borough of King's Lynn and West Norfolk and one by the Senate of the University of Cambridge). There were also to be three co-optative trustees, two of whom had to be women. The assets of the Trust were to be vested in the Official Custodian for Charities and the annual interest used for the benefit of girls living in the area formerly served by the High School. Girls at school or in the first years subsequent to leaving school or further education can apply for financial help towards, for example, professional or vocational training, an educational activity, study at home or abroad, training in music, sport or the creative arts, the provision of essential books or equipment and course fees. In 2011 the estimated value of the Trust's assets was in excess of £500,000 and the annual income to be disbursed is about £20,000.

In a report in the *Lynn News* in June 2004 following the death of Winifred Dore, aged 97, it was said that she 'revolutionised life at the High School when she arrived 60 years ago'. It is perhaps appropriate that we bring this book to an end with a report of a grand re-union held in 1985 which was the brain child of Miss Dore, although most of the organisation fell to Norah Howe-Smith. It was held on Sunday 2 June and was attended by some 500 former staff and students. The oldest person attending had left school in 1918 and the youngest in 1980. The King Street building was still used as the sixth-form centre for Springwood High School but they were about to move out and the building was to be sold to a private developer. This would be the last opportunity to see the old school before it was converted into the flats of Old School Court. After a lunch at the Duke's Head Hotel, Miss Dore, according to Val Hawkins (Jaggs), brought the house down by using almost the same words she had always said at the end of assemblies: 'Now girls, I want you to go quickly and quietly to the school.'

Miss Dore and Minnie Holden, the 1945 Queen's Prize winner, at the 1985 re-union (EDP)

Appendix 1.

Queen's Prize Winners 1887 to 1979

Princess Alexandra

1888 Gertrude Swann
1889 Helen Witt
1890 Florence Young
1891 Ethel King
1892 Mabel Howell
1893 Mabel Copley
1894 Katherine Swann
1895 Florence Swann
1896 Mildred Clayton
1897 Ethel Morgan
1898 Edith Soloman
1899 Agnes Green
1900 Edith Long
      Ellen Humphrey

Queen Alexandra

1901 Freda Gardiner
1902 Florence Morrison
1903 Dorothy Rolfe
1904 Grace Blackburn
1905 Florence Bloy
1906
1907 Winifred Coulton
      Freda Harbage
1908 Norah Spreckley
1909 Florence May Jarred
1910 Enid Vickers
1911 Dorothy Swithard
1912 Dorothy Chadwick
1913 Ruth Cross
1914 Rosamund Leeder
1915 Constance Parrish
1916 Mary Cross
1917 Edith Turner

1918 Doris Leeder
1919 Olive Hitchcock
1920 Dorothy Wolstencroft
1921 Ellen Feetham
1922 Joan Le Grice
1923 Margaret Ellison
1924 Dorothy Brown
1925 Alice Curzon

Queen Mary

1926 Olive Youngs
1927 Estella Beckett
1928 Dorothea Neale
1929 Margaret Dunwoody
1930 Margery Jary
1931 Emma Dorer
1932 Joan Hewitt
1933 Josephine Hamson
1934 Norah Bremner
1935 Phyllis Clarke
1936 Eleanor Dye

Queen Elizabeth

1937 Doreen Richer
1938 Pamela Sutherland
1939 Nora Mains
1940 Vera Richardson
1941 Marie Donaldson
1942 Betty Bromhead
1943 Jean Dunt
1944 Elizabeth Smith
1945 Minnie Drewery
1946 Jacqueline Shipp
1947 Marigold Colemen
1948 Mary Hewlett

1949 Marian Lake
1950 June Smith
1951 Beryl Elding
1952 Hilary Dodd
1953 Mollie Hammond
1954 Helen Daglish
1955 Bridget Bunting
1956 Ruth Coulton
1957 Diana Ducker
      Janet Turner
1958 Fay Cullum
1959 Brenda le Fleming-Jones
1960 Ann Kerkham
1961 Ronessa Fisk
1962 Diane Jaggs
1963 Marion Rout
1964 Vivien Browne
      Joy Waterworth
1965 Yvonne Bennion
1966 Margaret Hoare
1967 Lesley Thain
1968 Marian Smith
1969 Linda Fendley
1970 Diana Cousins
1971 Rosemary Morris
1972 Helen Horrex
1973 Sandra Cooper
1974 Jane Loasby
1975 Rosemary Talbot
1976 Susan Cross
1977 Valerie Green
1978 Kathryn Dryden
1979 Sally Bettinson

Note: There is some doubt about the prize winners in the years 1905 to 1908. The 1926 School Magazine lists no winners in 1906 and 1908 and has Winifred Coulton and Freda Harbage as joint winners in 1907. The 1962 Magazine replicates this. However the special 1985 publication has Freda as the winner in 1906, Winifred in 1907 and Norah Speckley in 1908. I have tried to marry the two above.

Appendix 2.

Queen's Prize Winners 1980 to 2011

Queen Elizabeth

1980	Karen McLennan
1981	Susan Large
1982	Joanne Coleman
1983	Ruth Marshall
1984	Alison Wiimore
1985	Robert Brown
1986	Laura Hawksworth
1987	Simon Dally
1988	Tony Smith
1989	Thomas Chapman
1990	David Fenra
1991	Andrew Cowling

1992	Lucy Woollatt
1993	Elizabeth Owen
1994	Alice Cason
1995	Bryn Probert
	Elizabeth Tomlinson
1996	Daniel Bloy
1997	Nicola Bartlett
1998	Sarah Howard
1999	Rebecca Howard
2000	Ewa Szypula
2001	Rosie Clift

Queen Elizabeth II

2002	Mark Lawrence
2003	Anna Williams
2004	Jennifer Howard
2005	Elizabeth Bartram
2006	Rebecca Edwards
2007	Fiona Hayter
2008	Christopher Stevens-Smith
2009	Samantha Fuller
2010	Daniel McGarry
2011	Jonathan Page

Appendix 3.

1932 whole-school photograph. (1)

1932 whole-school photograph. (2)

1932 whole-school photograph. (3)

1932 whole-school photograph. (4)

Appendix 4.

1947 whole-school photograph (1)

1947 whole-school photograph (2)

1947 whole-school photograph (3)

1947 whole-school photograph (4)

1947 whole-school photograph (5)

Appendix 5.

1966 whole-school photograph. (1)

1966 whole-school photograph. (2)

1966 whole-school photograph. (3)

& KING'S LYNN HIGH SCHOOL.

1966 whole-school photograph. (4)

Appendix 6.

1976 whole-school photograph (1)

1976 whole-school photograph (2)

1976 whole-school photograph (3)

1976 whole-school photograph (4)

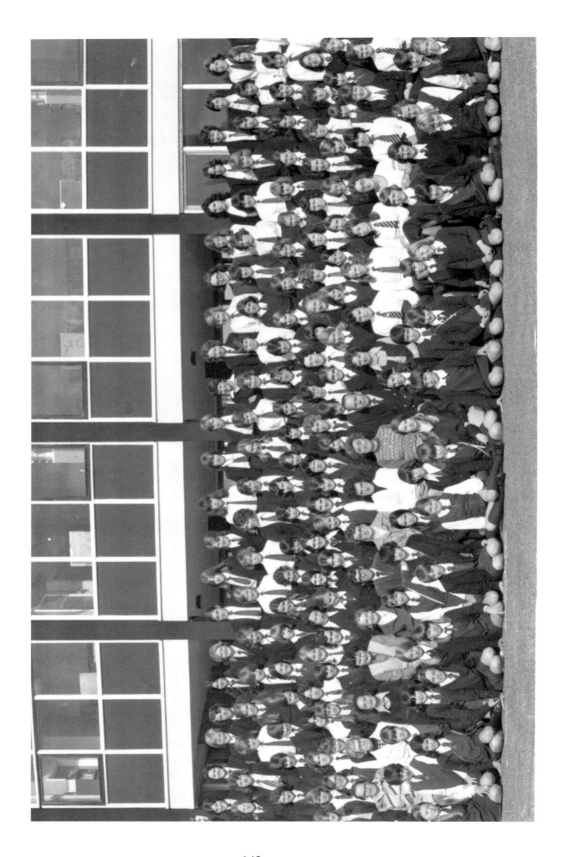

1976 whole-school photograph (5)

Index

Index

V